TO D

lou

M000233232

SUMMERS WITH SEVE

SUMMERS WITH SEVE

*My Life as
Severiano Ballesteros' Caddie*

IAN WRIGHT

with Jeff Connor

PELHAM BOOKS

PELHAM BOOKS

Published by the Penguin Group
27 Wrights Lane, London w8 5TZ, England
Viking Penguin, a division of Penguin Books USA Inc.
375 Hudson Street, New York, NY 10014, USA
Penguin Books Australia Ltd, Ringwood, Victoria, Australia
Penguin Books Canada Ltd, 2801 John Street, Markham, Ontario, Canada, L3R 1B4
Penguin Books (NZ) Ltd, 182–190 Wairau Road, Auckland 10, New Zealand

Penguin Books Ltd, Registered Offices: Harmondsworth, Middlesex, England

First published 1991
1 3 5 7 9 10 8 6 4 2

Copyright © Jeff Connor and Ian Wright, 1991

Printed in England by Clays Ltd, St Ives plc
Typeset in 11½/13½ pt Plantin

ISBN 0 7207 1988 7
A CIP catalogue record for this book is available from the British Library

Photo Acknowledgements
All photos by Matthew Harris except photo 1: Jan Traylen;
2: Bill Wynne; 13: North News and Pictures.

To
Seve and Carmen
for all the happy times together;
and to
Lesley and the boys
and all the friends
who made this book possible

Contents

I

Missing the Cut

On 11 August 1990, 35,000 feet above the Atlantic *en route* between Birmingham, Alabama, and London's Heathrow, I was seated with the man I will always consider the greatest golfer in the world. For the first time in my life I was travelling first class and was determined to enjoy it, because as I sipped a glass of champagne and took pleasure in the good company of Severiano Ballesteros, I knew it was possibly the last time too.

Seve, the superstar from Santander, and his employee of three seasons Ian Wright, the former insurance salesman (and quite a few other occupations) turned golf caddie from North Yorkshire, had decided that they were about to play their last tournament in partnership. The parting was to be amicable but saddening nevertheless, because in the previous two and a half years since Seve had taken me on as his caddie, I had shared a lot of his triumphs and even more of his disappointments. In that time I like to think I had become more than a caddie, perhaps even a good friend.

Employment with Seve had meant financial security for me and my family; Lesley and I had our own house after eighteen years of marriage and I was in the black for the first time in a long while. I had had a marvellous time, I'd travelled the world and met most of the game's top players, I had been alongside Seve for one major championship and eight other wins, and marvelled first hand at the genius and character and integrity of a man I was proud to call my boss. Now, as the plane sped on towards London, we both knew the relationship was over.

By rights on that Saturday we should still have been at Shoal Creek, Memphis, for the US PGA Championship, but almost inevitably, with Seve's form as it then was, we had missed the cut and were going home early. Seve was suffering through one of the worst slumps in his career and it had become almost commonplace for our interest in tournaments to end after two rounds while others, quite often less able, carried on for four days. As I had long anticipated, I was beginning to bear the brunt of his frustrations.

In my turn, I felt completely lost because there was nothing more I could do to help him. I'd done my best and kept trying, but nothing changed. Now it was actually costing me money to caddie for him since he was so far out of the prize money most of the time that there was no percentage for me.

Shoal Creek in many ways was the straw that broke the camel's back, although things had been moving rapidly to a head even before that. I had already been sacked and reinstated once that season and he had left me out of his plans for the British Open at St Andrews, preferring to let his older brother, Vicente, carry his bag, as he had in the past. But Shoal Creek was the time I finally cracked.

On the first day of the championship, which, like all US PGA titles, took place on a course perversely grown into as difficult a challenge as possible with some horrendous rough that ruined many a card that week, I had had a severe rollicking for not putting the flag back in the thirteenth hole quickly enough as Seve putted, and on the seventeenth he had blown up again when he put his ball in the water. It had to be my fault, of course, but whereas in the past I had just learned to keep quiet and take the medicine, this time I had had enough. On the way back to the hotel I had told him I didn't want to caddie for him the following day. All the frustrations and disappointments of the last twelve months went into that one decision: I had lost all heart. I was ready to commit the ultimate crime of a golf caddie and down tools on the spot.

A very shocked player tried to talk me round and in the end I calmed down, decided that I could not do the unforgivable and agreed to go out with him for the second round. But we both knew the end had come. After the second round on the Friday and the inevitable early finish, I picked Seve up in the courtesy car the day after, drove to the airport and embarked for home. Once we were settled down in the first-class cabin, dined (and wined in my case), we discussed the details of our 'divorce'. Like our first meeting three years earlier at Las Brisas, Spain, where he had first asked me to work for him, it was all done in a business-like way. For a start we weren't going to tell anyone that the NM English Open at The Belfry that week would be our last four rounds together; and we were going to try to go out with a win. Seve agreed that our parting was all for the best and we would remain good friends, and this was what I wanted – an amicable arrangement without rancour.

SUMMERS WITH SEVE

I'd had three glorious summers with Seve and as I sipped another glass of champagne and looked out of the cabin window on to a sea of cloud I could reflect on what I knew was the high point of my life. It hadn't always been like that, of course.

2

Jack of All Trades

ON THE GOLF CIRCUIT they call me 'Lucky' and I have to admit that good fortune has played a big part in my life. My wife Lesley calls me a gambler – which as a caddie you have to be, because you are gambling that your man is going to do well and win a few bob for you both. If he's going to miss every cut, you're going to go hungry, and I don't really want to feel hungry again.

When I took up bag-carrying for a living, I was flat broke. In fact I wasn't just broke: we were several thousand pounds in debt and I had no career and not much of a future. Lesley and I were living on a Redcar council estate with two growing lads to look after, and although I had had several jobs I hadn't stuck long at any.

Although I was born in Wythall near Birmingham, my roots are in Redcar (which the bureaucrats now say is Cleveland but which everyone else in the town will tell you is in Yorkshire). We moved up there when I was a year and a half old because my dad had got a job at the Wilton ICI plant that dominates life in the town. There were no golfers in the family but I've always been a sportsman. At school I was Northumberland and Durham diving champion and played Sunday League football for ICI Wilton on the right wing (19 goals in my best season). At one time I was North Yorkshire youth darts champion and even won a piano-smashing contest! We used to do daft things like that in those days.

I left school at fifteen to join the RAF. I'd wanted to train as an electrician but they took me in as an accountant, of all things. I'd been good at geography and maths at school and, looking back now, I suppose you couldn't have better qualifications to be a golf caddie because I spend half my life travelling the world and the other half trying to work out percentages. The RAF had told me I could change trades when I got in but they reneged on that and I bought myself out for £200.

I met my wife Lesley at the local discotheque when I was twenty-one and within five months we were married. She was dancing with some friends and I think I must have had a bit to drink because I walked her home that night and then told her to get rid of her boyfriend and it all snowballed from there. We lived at my Mum's for a spell, then we rented a maisonette in town before we got on the council house list. In the meantime along came the two lads and I found myself with four mouths to feed.

I tried all sorts of jobs. I spent four years at ICI in the nylon plant, had a spell out in Libya helping to commission gas plants, worked as a British Rail policeman and for British Steel, ran a driving school, and was even the local man from the Pru for a time. Even with all those jobs I still couldn't find anything I really fancied. To be honest I wasn't just going to take a job for the sake of it: I preferred being on the dole. Lesley had her part-time job as a hairdresser and with the unemployment money we'd get by – just. I'd had a couple of bank loans and with packing up work I'd arranged to pay a set amount each week. I'd sold the car to make ends meet but I was still deep in debt and although I wasn't totally unhappy I could see we were going nowhere fast.

Then, in 1983, and more out of desperation than anything else, I decided to have a go at caddying. I'd first tried my hand at golf three years earlier when Colin Cox, a colleague from the insurance company, said, 'Come and have a go.' Like so many, I tried it and got hooked. I went up and had a few lessons, bought a set of clubs and got down from 24 to 12 in no time at all with playing three or four times a week. I was proud to play in the rabbit section in those days and that to me was my best education in golf. In 1989 the other rabbits at Cleveland Golf Club honoured me with the presentation of a silver whisky flask and, in spite of everything else that happened that year, it remains one of the highlights for me.

On TV I'd watched the superstars like Trevino, Palmer, Watson and a young Seve – I'm a great TV sports watcher – without realizing that within a couple of years I'd be passing the time of day with them, standing on the same tee watching them swing, even discussing the weather and their families.

At Cleveland Golf Club I used to come into contact with Barry Stevens, a local pro, and Philip Harrison who was on the tour. Barry was the professional at Teesside Golf Club down the A19 from me at Thornaby and Philip, who lives in Carlisle, had been on the tour since 1979. Phil is a fitness fanatic who is also into boxing and soccer.

One day Barry said to me, 'Why don't you come and carry my bag in the Car-Care qualifying tournament in Leeds tomorrow?'

'Well, I don't know the first thing about caddying,' I said.

'It's your chance to start then,' came the reply. 'I'll pick you up at 6 am.'

'Six?'

'Yes, we can get some breakfast on the way.'

'OK, anything for a laugh.'

And that was how it started. I caddied for Barry in the morning, but unfortunately he failed to qualify. I was just thinking that was the beginning and the end of my caddying career when Phil pulled up as I was putting the clubs away.

'What on earth are you doing here?' he asked me.

'Well, I've just been carrying the bag for Barry Stevens, but we're on our way home now.'

'You must have a good idea of the course by now. Why don't you come and caddie for me this afternoon? I'll buy you lunch first.'

So there it was, 'payment' in advance and my career as a bag carrier was launched, although it didn't exactly start with a fanfare of trumpets. Phil got through the qualifier but already had a caddie arranged for the tournament itself. However, I managed to get fixed up with Donald Stirling, the Harrogate pro, by just walking up to him in the car park and asking if he wanted a caddie. Since then I've learned that many jobs are won and lost in car parks around the world's golf courses. After a practice round Donald told me what he expected from me for the next four days, but I was the rawest of beginners – I literally just walked along behind the player carrying his bag. I hadn't a clue what else to do.

Occasionally Barry or Phil would ask a bit of advice as anyone else would: 'Do you think it's this or that?' But whether my advice was any good or not, I don't know. All I was doing was saying what I thought at the time. That first afternoon with Phil I could at least tell him the shape of the holes and where the flags were, but it was Roy Holland, whom I met on the first tee after Donald had taken me on, who started my apprenticeship.

Roy was caddie to Brian Waites, the club pro noted for his achievements as an outsider in many a big tournament, and as I quizzed Roy at the Car-Care, he began to put me right on the dos and don'ts – like where to put the flag down, where to put the bag down, how to do your own yardages and where to measure from; and the art of saving yourself time, putting the bag down off the line of all the putts, then collecting it and heading off in the right direction. Where to stand with your player – that's important: you should be neither too close nor too far away, so that you can still talk to him and take the club. Every player has his own way on the golf course. Some like you to pick their clubs, others want to be told which ones to use. Some read their own lines on the green while others like the caddie behind to help out even though it's going to be their own decision ultimately.

I'm no different from anybody else and at first I made a lot of mistakes. I still do, even now – there's no way you stop making mistakes. Sometimes you can be concentrating so hard that you get in someone's way. One incident in the early days comes to mind.

I was caddying for Brian Marchbank from Gleneagles and we were paired with Bernhard Langer. Now in those days Bernhard was a very quick player. He was bunkered but I had it worked out that he would step into the bunker, get the feel of the sand, take a couple of practice swings and, while all this was going on, I'd have time to walk across the front of the bunker to where Brian was standing. I was half-way across and the next thing I knew the ball and some sand came flying out. I got a few choice words from Bernhard – and they weren't in German! – about being a bit more careful.

These are the things you learn as you go along. You learn which players play quickly and which slowly. Even now I'm still learning.

Roy helped me a lot in those early days and we've become very close friends since then. We're actually nicknamed 'the "A" team' because we travel together and room together. Roy is a very jovial little guy who lives on his nerves – we call him 'Skippy' or 'Jumpy'. He can have you up at 5am when he's got a 2pm start, because if his player is doing well and he's up in the top twenty, Roy likes to get there nice and early. To Jumpy that means, in most cases, three hours too early.

My first pay was £80 caddying for Donald Stirling and then I got £110 carrying for Graham Burroughs at Royal St Georges. Donald and Graham are your typical club professionals who got in by qualifying, but they both made all four days so the Wright luck was beginning to work. I was seeing the good side of things. I learned the cheapest way of getting around, usually by bus or train, and the cheapest places to sleep – the small hotels, bed-and-breakfasts or digs.

I got another big break at the end of 1983 when I met David Jones and started working for him, because he then went right out and made seven straight cuts in

PGA events and the only one we missed was the Open pre-qualifying. David, a big, genial Ulsterman from Newcastle, County Down, is known as 'the Long Fellow' because at 6 feet 5 inches he is the tallest man on the tour. He had turned pro in 1967 and qualified for the tour two years later. He is a golfer of ability as his round of 60 in the 1977 Ulster Championship showed, and he had also tied third in the Carroll's Irish Open at Portmarnock in 1981. From my point of view, David turned out to be just about the most gentlemanly person you could wish to meet. He taught me from the golfer's side what to do as a caddie, particularly about working out yardages, and it was David in the end who encouraged me to start my yardage book business.

I was still totally naive about the business at this stage, but I had the nerve to get on. At the end of 1983 I rang up Brian Marchbank, whose father Ian is the pro at Gleneagles Hotel, and asked him straight out: 'I know you haven't a caddie for the next year. How about taking me on?' He agreed, which was a huge bonus for me because Brian, who is a former British Boys and Youth champion, beating Sandy Lyle in the first championship, was a good, established player and to be seen with him all year was a big help to my own ambitions. Since his tour debut in 1979, Brian had climbed slowly up the prize-money list and in the previous year had finished thirty-eighth in the Order of Merit. Lucky Wright again . . . because if you were to pick a couple of golfers to start caddying for, David and Brian would be the choice, two of the nicest guys on the tour.

In the meantime, of course, I had to get through winter. When I signed on the dole, the girl behind the counter asked me what sort of job I did and was surprised when I replied: 'Golf caddying.' I don't think they'd had a caddie on the dole before and it opened a few eyes in Redcar, although my wife never told anyone what I did.

Lesley was concerned because we were only just surviving. I was getting by financially by the skin of my teeth, and with the boys still at school we just about kept afloat. Things were so bad that often when I went caddying I had to 'sleep' under canvas. I'd hop on a bus to the tournament venue with my tent and a sleeping bag, find a nice quiet spot on the course and pitch it and that was it – that was home for the week. It was a two-man tent and occasionally I'd be able to take in another caddie as a lodger. Quite often there would be a couple of other lads in tents alongside, making a sort of Caddie Camp, although it was far from a holiday most of the time. Meals would be a cheap dish of the day at the nearest cafe.

These were the caddies who were having a hard time and it was surprising how many of them there were. At times when the temperature got down to freezing and I was tired and cold and hungry and trying to sleep with my head tucked down inside the sleeping bag, I'd wonder what the hell I was doing there. But all the time I had this in-built confidence that said: 'Keep going, make it work.' This made me persevere, together with the fact that I really enjoyed the job and I could look at people like Peter Coleman, who carried for Langer, and Dave Musgrove, Sandy Lyle's regular caddie, and think that if they could do it so could I. All I needed was the luck and a bit of a break.

Dave and Peter were the caddie elite. They flew most places and stayed in reasonable accommodation, although in those days caddies at tournaments were not treated too well. It took a long time to break down the old rules and prejudices around the golf clubs. So while Dave and Peter were checking out at Heathrow, I'd be on a bus or in a train.

Take my first job of 1984 with Brian Marchbank. I had to get to Monza for the Italian Open. Simple! Bus from Redcar to Middlesbrough, bus from Middlesbrough to London, bus from London to Milan and train from there to Monza. I'd just look on the map and work out the cheapest way of getting there and off I'd go. Over the years, of course, I've graduated from public transport to flights almost everywhere and I now have a list of favourite accommodation in this country and abroad. A lot of the guest-house owners have become friends. In Scotland, for example, I will always try to stay with Bill and Christine Toms at Auchterarder, where Brian Marchbank lived, and my son Damon stays with them too, now.

In those early days I soon learned at first hand what a precarious existence a caddie's life can be and what a gamble I was taking. All the expenses come out of your own pocket so you're taking a risk that your man is going to do well. Success in caddying is making the cut for a start, then finishing as high as possible so you get your bit of percentage to boost the wages. Obviously Jack Nicklaus' caddie in his best years or Nick Faldo's caddie now don't have much to worry about in life.

A common thing among caddies when they're talking together is to say: '*We* played a good shot at the sixteenth, then we had a good putt on the seventeenth to make a birdie, but on the eighteenth *he* went and drove into sand!' That's human nature, but we do regard ourselves as part of a team. Strictly speaking, of course, it should be 'he' all the time.

When I was with Brian in 1984 we finished fourth at Haggs Castle near Glasgow, the nearest I'd come to a win with a player. I got really excited because, although Ken Brown finished out of sight on his own, we had a good chance at second last. But then we bogeyed seventeen and eighteen and slipped out of it. Brian hit his drive on seventeen into a bunker down the left and I think now, looking back and with a bit more experience, I'd have asked him to take an iron off the tee for position, but I was still a beginner then and kept quiet. Working with Seve later I learned to be more positive and not to be afraid to open my mouth, because the moment I haven't passed on information he's told me straightaway.

You have to learn to plan in advance and know all the danger areas, and that's where the team work comes in. But I was also to learn that even if you do everything right, some players will still blame the caddie when things go wrong.

3

Bag Man

EAMONN DARCY IS A BIG, raw-boned Irishman from Delgany with an unorthodox swing and the broken features of a boxer. He is probably best known for the putt on the eighteenth green at Muirfield Village, Ohio, that beat Ben Crenshaw and kept the Ryder Cup for Europe in 1987. When I went to work for him he was thirty-three and into hunting, shooting and fishing off the course. He had had some great years as a pro, coming third in the Order of Merit in 1975 and second in 1976, and with a win in the 1983 Benson and Hedges Spanish Open to his credit. He had played in three Ryder Cups up until then and getting his bag was a great capture for any aspiring caddie. On the surface Eamonn looks a genial sort of bloke, and when he asked me to caddie for him in 1985 I was quite pleased because here was a 'name' who wanted to employ me and it was the first time I'd been with one of the top fifty players on the European tour.

Now certain players have a reputation among caddies. Howard Clark is one I've never wanted to work with because while's as nice as pie off the course he becomes Mr Hyde on it. An absolute gent when he steps off the last green, on the course he puts on a werewolf mask. He has been very volatile with his caddies and undeservedly so at times. Probably the best thing Howard ever did was take on Fanny Sunesson as his caddie, since at least her presence probably cut down on some of his swearing. He must have had the same theory last year because after Fanny left him to go to Nick Faldo, I noticed Howard had Lindsay Anderson, the Scottish Ladies' Championship finalist in 1989, working for him in the Dunhill Cup at St Andrews. Perhaps Howard needs the calming influence of a woman to cool his fiery temperament.

When Darcy approached me I knew he had a similar reputation. He tended to have trouble keeping his caddies and was said to be very difficult and demanding, but my philosophy at the time was that you have to give these guys a go because until you see them at first hand you're never going to know exactly what they're like. It's no good just taking everything on hearsay; if I had listened to all the hearsay I would never have worked with Seve.

That's why after twelve months with Brian Marchbank I had decided to go freelance. I was still learning the trade and I had reasoned that the best way of learning was to work with as many different players as possible. However, Eamonn taught me one lesson I could have done without. I soon began to realize that if things started to go wrong with him, he'd blame me, even though he was playing lousy. He had to believe that his caddie was 'lucky' for him and it became very difficult to work with him. He was pretty tight on the shekels too – never a penny more nor a penny less, always the right amount regardless of how he'd done in the tournament.

But I was still astonished when, just a couple of days after telling me that I would be working for him in the Open, he announced he'd changed his mind and sacked me. We had just had a good tournament at The Belfry and with two days to go to the Open at Royal St Georges, Eamonn hauled me off into the car park and told me I was fired. I think he'd got it into his head that we weren't seeing eye to eye, and when a player starts thinking that it's probably time for a parting of the ways.

At the time I was looking forward to going into the Open with a really good player for the first time and with a chance to do well, but at that late stage there was little hope of picking up another bag. So here was another valuable lesson in my caddying apprenticeship: if something goes wrong, it's your fault and not the player's. Eamonn would vent his frustrations on me in no uncertain terms and I'd never know what was coming next. It brought home to me the real insecurity of the job I'd picked. I'm not the first and I won't be the last caddie to find this out the hard way.

In the winter of 1989 Andy Prodger had just had the best year of his career carrying Nick Faldo's bag. Andy is very experienced in his job and, like the rest of us, knows how things can go wrong in a relationship and what a tightrope you walk as a caddie. But it still came as a hell of a shock when Nick sacked him. It shook us all, because you just don't expect it after having a good year with a player. You expect success to strengthen the relationship between caddie and player, and normally you can tell when things are not going so well and when to half-expect the boot. You learn to read the signs, but Andy's sacking was like a bolt from the blue and left us all with, shall we say, food for thought. One minute you're up there on the TV screens carrying the bag of an Open winner and the next you're on the dole, because there are no written contracts between player and caddie. It's all done on a handshake, although I will say that golfers are the most honourable of men and there's a lot of integrity, particularly among the old school.

It was Maurice Bembridge, one of the long-established players, who came to my rescue after Darcy had fired me. Maurice, an affable and easy-going Midlander, had been around since 1960 and although he was past forty when he gave me a job, was still capable of some marvellous golf. In his heyday he was as good as anyone in the world for a round or two and his 63 in the Open qualifying of 1967 still equals the lowest ever. In 1974 he had stunned the Americans by reducing the Augusta Masters to something akin to a pitch-and-putt course with a last-round 64, tying the record. A Ryder Cup player four times, including in the famous tied match at Birkdale in 1969, he had also finished fifth in the British Open of 1968.

Losing Darcy's bag was a major setback, but Maurice stepped in and I carried for him in the Open qualifying. If there was a caddie going spare, a lot of the older players would take him out of etiquette, and I'll never forget that gesture from Maurice. I used to sit and listen to the tales of him and his big mate Eddie Polland and the battles they had with the great players, the anecdotes; how he had once played Jack Nicklaus twice in a day in the Ryder Cup and managed to half in the morning only to lose by two holes in the afternoon. It was an experience for me just hear the stories.

Unfortunately, after Maurice qualified, the wind got up at Royal St Georges and blew us all over the course. Maurice wasn't the biggest hitter in the world and St Georges is extremely long, so it was a case of packing the bags, going home and wondering whom I was going to work for next.

Fortunately, by this time, I did have another string to my bow. It was big David Jones who had encouraged me to start making yardage books, and it was this more than anything else, I suppose, that put my name on the map around the circuit. I'd got to one course with David and he had suggested that I draw him a book of the course by hand because he reckoned it would save him measuring it. He could just turn up any time and not worry about pacing out the yardages: obviously, if a player can land in any part of any course and know exactly how far he has to go to the green, he can just pick the appropriate club out of the bag and fire away.

In those days my books were horrible things. I'd draw nine holes on one side of a sheet of foolscap paper – just a rough picture, desperate compared with what my books are now, but it did the job for the player and he could just take the sheet round the course with him. I used to cut up the sheets with a pair of scissors and staple them together. If it rained, of course, they tended to disintegrate! Pretty soon they got a bit more sophisticated with six holes on A4 paper, and then I really got sophisticated with a little wheel for measuring and a paper guillotine instead of the scissors. I'd start by drawing each hole and measuring the distance from the tee to the traps or other dangers. The PGA put out yellow and red dot markers to help save time and stop caddies or players marking the fairways, and I'd measure the yardage to these dots, then from there to the front of the green and sketch them in on the drawing. At first it would be just a base drawing, not to scale but making sure that everything was in proportion, and then I'd go out on the course and draw in the detail, working out where the most likely landing places for shots were and measuring from there.

If nothing else it kept me very fit, because with all the to-ing and fro-ing I'd be walking about 7 or 8 miles a day, usually at 6am, and then have to go out and do my round with the player. I'd have to find a quiet time to do the drawing, so most mornings I'd be out there with my wheel making lines in the dew. I'd do eighteen holes with the player, then I'd be sat up until two in the morning stapling some more paper together. Eventually the bits of paper developed into a little book, and soon most of the top pros or their caddies were asking me for a copy at tournaments and I was in business.

At the start I charged £2, then it went up to £3.50 (inflation!). It seems unreal, but there was Ian Wright from Grosmont Close, on a Cleveland council estate, taking three quid off Greg Norman or Sandy Lyle or Bernhard Langer for a little book of paper held together by staples and saying, 'Ta very much, very nice to do business with you!' But at least I wasn't living in the tent any more and I was developing a higher profile among the top professionals.

I was getting a few more stamps in my passport by now too. An average start to the year would be Cannes, Madrid, Italy, a week off to see if the kids had grown any more, then it would be back to Madrid, to Wentworth, Moor Park, Woburn, Sweden and Monte Carlo. It may sound glamorous, but like a lot of things that sound glamorous there's often a major drawback. The travelling is the big killer. If your player makes all four days, you finish a tournament on a Sunday night then climb on a train at 6.30, going, say, from Madrid to Italy, so you're there in time to do the yardages on the Monday ready for the player reappearing on the Tuesday. In the early days it was all train or coach – I couldn't afford the air fare – although occasionally I'd thumb a lift with a player. Once I travelled with Chris Moody to Holland on the ferry from Hull. Then over to Stockholm, back to York, up to Scotland, across to Dusseldorf, then to Switzerland, back to Sunningdale, then to The Belfry and finally up to St Andrews for the Dunhill Cup: a hitch hiker's ride to the golfing galaxy!

And still the learning process went on. I learned that at the La Turbie course in Monte Carlo or Cranssur-Sierre in Switzerland you take one club less than normal because you are on top of a mountain and the ball flies a lot further in the thin air. I learned to take into consideration the wind and whether it's a warm or a cold wind, because that affects the way a ball flies, and I learned to keep charts of each player and how far he hit with each club under normal conditions. I also kept my eye open for a star of the future to whom I could perhaps hitch my wagon.

It was in the early 1980s that a number of young Swedish golfers started appearing on the scene. They were all good players, and the buzz round the caddie circuit was they were good payers too. What's more, they all spoke perfect English and were perfect gents. Like a lot of Scandinavians they were very keen on keeping fit and most of them had their individual training schedules.

I'd seen Magnus Persson around for some time and he had always impressed me. I saw a lot of potential in him and I could envisage him winning tournaments before long. He's a smallish guy at about 5 feet 7 inches and just over 10 stone, very quiet, dedicated and always willing to work at his game. When I went to work for him he was only twenty-one and looked even younger, but in fact had already been on the tour for three years, starting off at eighty-seventh in the Order of Merit in 1983, his first year on tour, and heading upwards. For a small man Magnus hit the ball a long way and I could see the prospect of a few top-ten finishes for any caddie working with him. So, in my usual shy, retiring way, I just went up to him on the putting green one day and asked him straight out. He put me on a trial basis and we finished up with almost two years together, although I did work for others in between. He also allowed me to continue with Ian Wright Yardage Books Ltd, which had become very important to me. The books had become established by now: there were sixty or seventy pros a week – the hard core of the leading players – taking them at different tournaments and it was almost doubling my wages. It meant that I could fly around to tournaments as well as start to pay off some of my debts at home. Magnus looked after me very well and although we never got a win we had several very good finishes.

Up to that point I'd had eight or nine second places and every other place up to tenth with players from all over the place, and when I did first get a win it was with a pro who lived only 30 miles from my home! David Llewellyn is a roly-poly, comic character who was born in Kent, plays for Wales and lives in Thirsk, North Yorkshire. Known as 'Lu-Lu' on the circuit, he is an unconventional sort who had tried everything to improve his game. When he approached me for the Robert Sangster Vernons Open at Hoylake in 1987, he had slipped from a year of high earnings of over

£46,000 in 1985 to seventieth place in the Order of
Merit in 1986 when he had struggled to earn £18,000.

Always one to experiment, David had even dropped
off the tour altogether at one time to take a club job in
Malta, and was then a regular client of Alan Fine, the
sports psychologist. One of the theories was that you
should take your mind off golf between shots, so
David was always quietly singing to himself on the
way up the fairway. Whatever he was singing, he was
playing our tune, because we quietly got into contention without doing anything spectacular and by the
last hole had a one-shot lead. We had a par to make
and we did. It was a terrific feeling as it had come quite
unexpectedly at the end of the year, and it was David's
first victory too. I've got a nice picture of us both
with the trophy and I thought at the time: 'That's
number one out of the way; now maybe my luck is
really changing.'

But you could have knocked me over with a feather
when one day, out of the blue, I was asked to caddie
for Severiano Ballesteros.

4

Meet the Maestro

DOWN AT CLEVELAND GOLF CLUB they used to pull my leg about my caddying ambitions. 'When are you going to caddie for Seve?' they used to ask. It was their way of keeping my feet on the ground, not letting me get too big-headed, because obviously I'd been on TV and in the Press by now and was a bit of a local personality. Like them I regarded the prospect of working with Ballesteros as pure fantasy.

I'd first seen Seve in the flesh back in 1985 when I was caddying for Vicente Fernandez in the Epson Matchplay at St Pierre, Chepstow, and Seve had come out for a practice round with Vicente who was his big mate. They made an odd combination, the tall, handsome Spaniard and the tiny Argentinian who had been born with one leg shorter than the other and had walked with a limp ever since – not that it ever affected his golf, as his thirteen tournament victories had showed.

I knew a lot about Ballesteros, of course: how he'd been born one of five sons to a fisherman in Pedrena, near Santander in northern Spain; all the famous stories about playing with a stick and stones on the local beach, becoming a professional at sixteen and then going on to become one of the greatest players ever. Watching him playing with Vicente, I could see why he was the best in the world just from the way he struck the ball, although I was doing my best to concentrate on my job for the day, which was caddying for Fernandez. I didn't speak to Seve then, but I had a long chat with Nick de Paul, the American who was his caddie at the time and who had brought him in at St Andrews for his second Open win in 1984.

Vicente was the go-between late in 1987 when Seve decided he wanted me to carry his bag. We were in Las Brisas, Spain, and I was caddying for Magnus when the first approach came. Like so much other golf business, the conversation took place in the course car park.

Vicente came straight down to it: 'Do you want to caddie for Seve?'

'Pardon?'

'Seve can't approach you directly himself because obviously he couldn't be seen to be poaching another player's caddie – it's not etiquette – but I've recommended you. I think you'll do a good job for him.'

Now, it's tremendous for a player to say that about a caddie, and my head was whirling because I had just never thought I was in that company or class.

I answered, 'Yes, but let me talk to Magnus about it first. I can't just go and talk to Seve.'

Magnus was great about it.

I said, 'Look, Seve's interested in me going to work for him. Do you mind if I talk to him?'

It took him by surprise but Magnus replied, 'Sure you can – you don't often get a chance like that.'

I hurried off to find Seve and met him on the practice ground. He took my name and address and asked whom I had caddied for, although knowing what I know now I realize he knew all that anyway. It was all short, sharp and to the point, and my impression was of a man who knew what he wanted in life and just got on with it. We shook hands and he said he'd be in touch.

I went back to Magnus and we just carried on. Funnily enough, after that Magnus started having some of his best results, but then he decided that we would split up as he thought my talk with Seve had had an unsettling effect on our relationship which of course it had. The winter of 1987 came and went and still there was no word from Seve. I thought, 'Well, I need to keep working and I can't keep waiting forever.' In an effort to find a more permanent job I fixed up to do the 1988 season with Carl Mason on a full-time basis.

Carl is a nice, easy-going guy from the Derbyshire Peak District who has been on the circuit for quite a while, an established player who turned pro in 1973 following a win in the British Youth Championship. In 1974 he had been rookie of the year, but since then he had gained a reputation for coming second, with five finishes as a runner-up between 1976 and 1987. I got on well with him and basically I'd had to shove the Seve thing to the back of my mind and concentrate on working with my new employer.

It was while I was working for Carl that I got my second tournament win in the weirdest of circumstances, another of those daft things that happen in golf. We were at El Prat, Barcelona, in March for the Torras Hostench Open and Carl had missed the cut. I was sitting down outside the clubhouse enjoying a bit of sun when David Whelan, who lived at Seaton Carew about 10 miles from my home in Redcar, came up pushing his own trolley. David is a big lad from Wearside with an interest in Sunderland soccer and it was his first year on tour. He'd been to the players' school in La Manga half a dozen times trying to get a card and finally he had succeeded. Barcelona was his second PGA tournament and he had missed the cut in the first. He was so hard up his dad had loaned him the air fare to get out to Barcelona and the money for his hotel bills. But at El Prat he had shot a 68 and a 65 and was leading when he came up and asked me what I was doing.

I said, 'I'm off home. I'm fed up – we've missed the cut.'

'Come and caddie for me for the last two rounds,' he said. 'I need a friend just to come round with me.'

I agreed, and after seventy-two holes we ended up in a four-way tie for the lead alongside Mark Mouland, Barry Lane and Nick Faldo: not a bad line-up. They've all won tournaments since and one of them has had quite a good couple of years!

David whittled them down one by one on the play-off. At the opening sudden-death hole both Faldo and Mouland missed birdie putts and David sank a 25-footer to match the two from Lane. At the fourth hole David's four finally beat Lane's five and he'd won the tournament and £33,000. I don't think David has played the same way since and his following season was something of a nightmare with a total of twelve missed half-way cuts in fifteen PGA events. But those two days at El Prat will always be a treasured memory for me and really confirmed that I was on a lucky roll.

Carl's win in the Sunningdale Foursomes the week after made it two in a row and I was thinking, 'Not a bad start to the year, Ian!' Then, on 18 April, I set off for Spain and the Madrid Open. I'd managed to put Seve out of my mind, although earlier in the season Steve Williams, who caddied for Greg Norman at the time, had told me there was a rumour going round America that I was caddying for Seve and that he was going round telling everyone just that.

I said, 'Well, that's funny, because he hasn't said anything to me.'

But then at Madrid I was sitting in the clubhouse having a snack – Carl was a few feet away with a group of other players – when Seve strode in. He came right over to where I was sat and asked, 'Are you working for Carl?'

Now, with Carl sitting there, I wasn't liable to say anything else but: 'Yes. I agreed to work for Carl for this year.'

Seve just turned round and walked straight out and I thought, 'That's torn it.'

I followed him out about twenty minutes later and found him sitting in the locker room.

I said, 'Right, now let's talk.'

Seve looked up and came right down to it. 'I want to take you on for a four-week trial,' he announced. Straight down to business again, the way I like it. I said I was interested and asked him about wages and percentages. They sounded all right, although like every other caddie I would have to find my own air fares and foot my own hotel bills.

'If you come through, you'll get all the Majors,' he said. 'Your trial starts at the PGA at Wentworth, then we'll be going to the French Open, Monte Carlo and the British Open.'

He didn't crack a smile or anything: it was pure business. We shook hands and that was that. I was

Seve Ballesteros' caddie. I rang Lesley at home in Redcar that night and told her. She couldn't believe it; neither could I in a way.

But this was just the start of the fairy story.

5

Smile, Seve, Smile

W HEN SEVE BALLESTEROS took me on as his caddie
at the start of 1988 he was thirty-one years old. He was
arguably *the* golfer of the decade, with two British
Opens, two US Masters and at least one title to his
credit every year since 1976, when he had won the
Dutch Open, his first tournament. In 1988 he was to
marry his childhood sweetheart Carmen, daughter of
the president of the local bank in Santander, but as far
as golf went had been without a Major since 1984. In
1987, in fact, he had just the Suze Open to his credit,
not a healthy state of affairs for a man who thrives on
being number one, whose whole life is governed by a
driving ambition to be the best.

In that time Seve had used a number of caddies
including, latterly, his brother Vicente. I think that
when he approached me he had decided to go back to
having a regular caddie in an effort to settle himself
down a little. On the course he had begun to look
careworn, as if he carried all the worries of the world
on his shoulders. These were my theories, but naturally

I kept them all to myself. I never asked why, I never wanted to know why. I was just concerned with getting on and doing the job for him.

Having said that, it was common sense, now that I had the bag, to ask around for some advice, because forewarned is forearmed and I knew he had the reputation for eating his caddies for breakfast. Peter Coleman, Bernhard Langer's caddie, had had a spell with Seve and he told me I'd find it very difficult. I was warned that I'd get the blame for everything including the wind making the grass move – even if the wind wasn't blowing! I talked to Dave Musgrove, who had carried Seve's bag in his 1979 Open victory at Royal Lytham, and his advice was simple: 'Don't take the job, Ian – you don't know what you're letting yourself in for.'

I have to admit that all this made me wonder a little, but when I sat down and thought about it I reasoned that I had been recommended for the job for the way I caddied and for being myself, so all I could do was carry on the same way. By the time May and Wentworth came around, the waiting had killed most of my nerves.

The PGA is a regular tour event and Wentworth has become one of our favourite courses over the years. On this occasion I stayed with an old friend who lives about half an hour away. I like my accommodation to be away from the course, because if you're staying nearby, especially in England, you can't go for a quiet drink at night without getting into golf conversations. As with any other job, when you've finished work for the day you want a break from golf 'shop'. Obviously, once I got more established with Seve that became more and more impossible because there always seemed to be someone who recognized me and wanted to ask this and that.

I'd arranged to meet my new boss on the Tuesday at 9am and, as always, I got there about an hour early to do a few jobs and pick up the odd guest badge for a friend. Seve arrived about 9.30, shook my hand, asked how I was and we set straight out for practice.

I'd rehearsed what I was going to ask him about his likes and dislikes, if there was anything I needed to know. In Seve's case, however, it wasn't necessary, for as soon as we set off down the first he turned round and said, 'Right, this is how I like things done.' He ran through the basics, like where he wanted the gloves and balls kept. Some players like them at the top of the bag, others at the back, so that if the caddie is doing a yardage and the player wants something out of the bag he knows exactly where to find it without having to rummage around. Certain players want to wander round on their own; others, like Seve, want you to keep up with them all the time.

Then we set off. If there's a *Guinness Book of Records* best for the quickest practice rounds at Wentworth, I'd like to enter 18 May 1988, because our round that day would be hard to beat. I couldn't believe we were moving that quickly. He just said, 'Call out the yardage, pick a club and I'll play it. I think I know the course quite well by now.'

By the twelfth we had passed Ken Brown and his caddie, 'Laughing Boy', and as we wafted past at speed I shouted out, 'I feel like the hare and the tortoise, and guess who's the tortoise!'

Seve didn't say very much, just asked occasionally about club selection and told me what he wanted around the greens. He told me where he wanted the bag, how he wanted the ball cleaned quickly – all the basics you have to take in on the first day.

When we got round to sixteen he slowed down a bit and it was there he started to talk about me personally.

'You seem to keep yourself in good shape. How old are you?'

I told him that I was thirty-nine, coming up to forty.

'Do you smoke?'

'No.'

'That's good. Do you drink?'

'Not really, just the occasional glass of wine with a meal.'

He nodded in approval and I decided it was perhaps time I said something.

'Do you know what keeps me young?' I asked him.

'No, what?'

'Sex!'

He just looked at me and I added, 'Well, it is 200 calories a jump,' and he burst out laughing.

I think that was when the ice was broken. I relaxed a lot more after that and as Seve chuckled while we walked on I felt the relationship started there. Since then some of my Yorkshire jokes have come in quite useful in tense situations. It's important to talk about something other than golf from time to time and I've used the odd crack to lighten things up if he has got too intense.

We finished the round – I remember the time exactly as two hours ten minutes – and to this day I believe he was testing me for speed and fitness and to see if I could keep up with him. I sat back that night and thought, 'I quite enjoyed that.' I had been nervous and a bit wary, because as far as I was concerned I was working for the world's number one player now and would be caddying on a different level altogether.

Concentration had to be 150 per cent – he told me that at the start.

I soon began to learn what sort of man I was working for. Seve is a driving perfectionist with the most incredible will to win. He is a different class of player from the other pros I had worked with so far, a different class in the shots he makes. There is also his general attitude to the game and his professional approach. Some of it began to rub off on me.

The day after practice we had the Pro Am. We had Terry Wogan with us, although I had a job to do and I couldn't afford to get starstruck. I am probably the world's worst Pro Am caddie as I tend to wander round making notes for the tournament – trying to finalise the plan of campaign, if you like – whereas Seve was all fired up wanting to win the Pro Am. Even later on I tended to use Pro Am days as a chance to do some extra homework and Seve would be always chuntering on at me about not being where he liked me to be.

The PGA itself went really well. We finished joint second – and even at this early stage Seve was starting to use 'we' when he was talking about playing shots – and I made a big impression with the family and friends back home when I became an accidental TV star. We were on the eighteenth in the third round and the cameras were on us. We had a little wait for the second shot and I forgot that there was a microphone close by. It all came out loud and clear on television.

Seve said, 'What club shall we hit, Ian?'

'Two iron,' I replied, and he went over and stood over the ball.

He said, 'Are you sure?

'Yes, a good positive shot.'

Apparently that proved a big talking point back

home at the golf club and the workies' club, because nobody thought that in my first week with the best golfer in the world I'd be giving him advice.

In the fourth round we got into a position to win the tournament and needed two birdies out of the last six holes to tie for the lead. On the seventeenth he knocked a good shot down to the side of the green, leaving a simple chip. Now Seve's well known for his short game and I couldn't believe it when he duffed the chip. So we finished par, par and in second place. Not a bad start, even though I felt he should have won it.

At Chantilly Seve arrived back jet-lagged from the USA and didn't perform well at all, and then at Monte Carlo we again got in a good position to win with four holes to go. But then we had a bad bogey at the shortest par four, the fifteenth, hitting the drive way left and under a rock. That bogey put us out of contention, because Mark McNulty and Jose Rivero made birdies and we finished third.

Seve and I seemed to have hit it off and I had reason to feel I was giving satisfaction. At an early stage he had spent half a day telling me dos and don'ts when he suddenly stopped and said, 'Ian, the reason I am giving you advice and saying all these things to you is hopefully to make you one of the best caddies in the world. Maybe *the* best caddie in the world.' Now this took me a bit aback, but it seemed fair enough. Seve had had some of the best caddies around and I knew then that I wasn't anywhere near the standards he required. But the fact that I was willing to listen and learn and take everything in, learning from mistakes and learning from my player, made all the difference.

However, I thought that there were ways I could help him too. So far I'd seen none of the famous

Spanish temperament: he had been quite relaxed and I think that's what he really wanted, what he saw as the key to getting back to where he belonged – on top. One day he asked me if there was anything I had to say to him, any advice, and I replied, 'I'd like to see you smile a bit more. I think that's what most people would like to see, because if you're smiling you're relaxed and you're going to produce your best swing.' Like everybody else would, he listened to the advice.

Then, just after Monte Carlo and a week before the British Open, Seve started talking about tournaments and venues later in the year. I thought this must mean: 'Forget the trial period', and I went to Lytham knowing that if there is such a thing as a steady job in the world of golf caddies, I had it.

Back home in Redcar there was some disbelief and some admiration, I suppose, because my friends had seen me through all the bad times and now it looked as though I had turned the corner. The reaction among the other caddies was more mixed. Initially there had been the feeling that I wouldn't last five minutes with Seve and there was even a book running that I wouldn't survive one or two weeks. I wish I'd been a bookmaker because I'd have made a few bob. There was a bit of jealousy, too, because I'd moved so quickly to a top bag. Some of them had been around for fifteen or twenty years and were still struggling. Later on, when the successes really started, some of the jealousies came spilling out. The majority of the top caddies understood. David Musgrove, Andy Prodger and Peter Coleman were smashing to me. They gave me a lot of support and a lot of help, and the sixty years' experience they had between them were a real benefit to me, but others were less than pleased.

The resentment was heightened as well in some

cases because I don't mix a lot with other caddies, I don't go out drinking or socialize with them. I like to think it's part of my professional attitude. I have a few friends like Roy and I still talk to the others – I'd never ignore them – but when you're working with a top player it's subtly different. Seve had hinted to me that I would be in the public eye a great deal once I joined up with him and I realized I had an image to keep up for him: if I was found staggering around all over the place he would not be too pleased. In fact, I wouldn't have kept the job.

Tour players may look on caddies as their right arm, but the same unfortunately doesn't hold true in a lot of clubhouses and when you arrive at some events it's still common to see the signs go up on a Tuesday: 'NO CADDIES ALLOWED'! The old-style caddie, we all admit, had a bad reputation, but times have changed and caddies have changed with them. So it is upsetting to find no-go areas at tournaments. Space is often limited, but caddies are human beings and if a player wants to take his caddie for lunch it should be allowed. At some places you can't even get a cup of tea or a sandwich at lunchtime and it's ridiculous when a caddie has perhaps half an hour to snatch something to eat to expect him to queue for refreshment with members of the public. Volvo have made a big effort with separate facilities for caddies and certain other tournaments have come round a bit, but at some places you can still be treated worse than a dog. You are corralled, you are not allowed to walk anywhere, you are not allowed in the pro's shop and you're not allowed in the stands where you might expect your player to turn up. Players like you in the locker room to fetch or change their shoes, but quite often that's not allowed either.

Then we are forced to wear those horrible white

overalls for four days like painters and decorators – we have even had letters from the Ministry of Health about them. It would be quite simple to have our own gear with sensible jackets and different-coloured trousers, perhaps with a sponsor's name on, because – let's face it – many caddies are as high-profile as the players these days. When you work for a top player you are photographed a lot, so you are virtually a walking advertising hoarding – though, in my opinion, too cheap. Most caddies have their own deals now, and if you work at it there is a lot of clothing sponsorship around. Anyone can be turned out well for play.

I met my first sponsor in 1988. I was wandering around Gleneagles doing my yardage books when I bumped into John Hales, head man at Titleist at the time, who asked me if I would wear the Wolsey range of sweaters and shirts. He said I looked like a male model! That was my first formal sponsorship and the following year I came to a deal with Mike Smith of Slazenger. They supply the towels, bags and gloves for Seve in Europe, and for a lump sum Slazenger agreed to supply me with clothing, shirts and visors. At the time it was a bit of breakthrough; personally I don't think a caddie should agree to wear any named product if he isn't paid.

Footjoy now supply the Caddies' Association with trainers twice a year, and as a result the bulk of the caddies on the circuit have no excuse for not walking about in comfort and style. Sunderland Waterproofs, through a genial guy called Stan Segal, make sure I'm kept dry most of the time and also give a caddie a good, smart image alongside the player. In 1990 I arranged another deal with Jochen Holley and Mike Spatz of Hugo Boss, whom I'd met at the Pro Am in the German Masters, for clothing and visors. Funnily enough, Boss didn't actually make visors and I had to have them all made up myself back in England. There were only about fifty ever made so they are as highly prized as a Pirelli calendar now – collectors' items!

If there are characters among the players, there are certainly characters among the caddies too. The best-known are probably Pete Coleman with his curly perm, Andy Prodger, who was sacked by Faldo, and Dave Musgrove. These are the cream, the best around. It's nice to see Pete reaping some reward lately for his loyalty to Bernhard Langer. He had been through a rough spell and there was a time when basically he wasn't making any money – he even had to sell his Porsche! It's hard for a caddie to stay with a player through the bad times, waiting for the good times to come back, and Pete would obviously have had his doubts about whether he was doing the right thing. But he hung in there with Bernhard and never changed, and his decision has been vindicated, which is nice for him because he is a family man now.

Steve Williams, who was fired by Greg Norman, is, at the time of writing, over in America with Raymond Floyd and doing quite nicely. He is into racing saloon cars and I get to hear the full story of his 'investments' from time to time. Steve had to part with Norman because Greg fancied a spell with Bruce, Tom Watson's old caddie, but I think he was probably secretly relieved because Greg was giving him a lot of stick. However, he did very well out of Greg.

There's also a guy called 'the Professor' who has a degree in law and who keeps us all entertained with magic tricks. 'Barry the Judge' is so called because he knows everything about everything, and then there's 'the Vicar' whose nickname was given him because he is the complete opposite! Phil Morbey, who caddies for Ian Woosnam, is known as 'Wobbly' for reasons that are obvious when you watch him walk. I see him quite a bit at the races, Wetherby or York. He had a great year in 1990 and managed to treat himself to a Ford Sierra Cosworth to get to and from tournaments more quickly. I'm known as 'Lucky' these days but it used to be 'Two Bags' because once I was caddying for someone whose mate's caddie hadn't turned up and I started pulling the mate's trolley just as we passed the clubhouse, inspiring a caddie called 'Rick the Rattler' to shout out: 'Two Bags!' That was how it started. I had done it for perhaps two holes, but the name stuck and spread from there. 'Rick the Rattler' was well known before he left the tour; he used to stand there and shake the clubs without realizing it – hence his nickname.

Harry Toan, the Irishman who caddied for David Feherty, goes back a long way with me. I remember he once tented with me back in the bad old days at Crans, and after a few drinks we tried to walk off the mountain in the fog which wasn't a good idea because there are some very big precipices on that course. It was more by good luck than good judgement that we staggered back to the tent in one piece.

The young Swedish woman Fanny Sunesson caused a bit of a stir when, after working with Howard Clark for a spell that included the Ryder Cup at The Belfry, she landed Nick Faldo's bag and instant fame and fortune, although she wasn't the first female caddie on the circuit. Tony Charnley's Dutch wife, Lucienne, who tours with Tony in a caravan, caddies for him and Tony hasn't done badly over the years. There was also a New Zealand girl around for a time. Fanny seems to be doing a very good job for Nick and she has some company now because, as mentioned earlier, Howard

Clark now has Lindsay Anderson from Lossiemouth with him.

I've also got to know some of the American caddies in my travels. At the Ryder Cup there were a few friendly wind-ups, particularly when some of them turned up in jeans, and the British boys took great delight in pointing out their lack of dress sense, but all in all it was quite good-natured and they are a smashing bunch. There are characters over there too. There's 'Squeaky' who used to caddie for Fred Couples, so called because of his high-pitched voice, and 'Boats' who is with Curtis Strange: if you saw his feet, you'd realize why they had inspired such a name! 'Fluff', who has a great walrus moustache, carries the bag for Peter Jacobsen. I've always found the American caddies very organized and extremely helpful and friendly.

The image of caddying has improved a lot, of course. There are still obviously one or two who like a drink, but it's not as it used to be. There are more and more young lads coming into the job now, lads with a professional attitude who realize that they have the chance of making a living and enjoying themselves at the same time. For the top twenty or thirty it is a very good living, but drifting down below that most of them just get by, as I did at one time. There are only a few married caddies – and even fewer with children – and it's even harder for them.

As in any job when you're away from home for long periods, there are times when I've sat in the hotel on my own and wished Lesley or the kids had been there. Like I said, I tend to steer clear of other caddies away from the course, and naturally caddies don't socialize with players. That's the way it has to be in golf. You can be friends with your player, but you can't afford to get too close or you might start carrying the relationship on to the golf course and then you wouldn't do your job properly – you'd relax too much. You must make a conscious effort to keep that gap because he is there to do a job and you're there to do a job and it has to be done professionally.

The more I caddied for Seve and the further I travelled, the more I realized how much class he had, how much talent, how much genius. And how much integrity. Golf is probably easier to cheat at than most other sports, but all players abide by the rules. There's a lot of honour in the game and Seve's sense of it is very strong. Like so many others he was brought up in the old school of discipline and fair play.

At one tournament in Germany we were playing the first hole on the last day and Seve knocked his putt up close, about a foot from the hole. We were playing with Des Smyth and we all set off to tidy things up. I picked up the flag and Seve knocked the ball in the hole. We were walking back to the bag when Seve caught me up and said, 'That was a six, Ian.'

I was flabbergasted: 'It was a five, wasn't it?'

'It was a six. I double-hit the putt.'

What had happened was that he'd put the putter behind the ball, moved it, then knocked it in. Nobody saw it – not his playing partner, not me, not anybody else. So I just went quietly up to Des and told him it was a six. That's how honest Seve is and that's how honest golf is.

On the course his shot-making just took my breath away. Sometimes I couldn't have imagined in my wildest fantasies how he could play a shot. He just saw things others wouldn't even dream about. And all the time I had this privileged armchair view of the man in action. I felt there was nothing Seve couldn't accomplish, and within two months of our agreeing to work together I was to watch him snatch the greatest prize of all.

6

Open Warfare

My first British Open had been in 1984 at St Andrews, ironically the scene of Seve's last Major. I was working for Brian Marchbank at the time and it was obviously something special being with Brian at the home of golf, seeing the enormous crowds and all the famous players I'd idolized over the years.

I remember when, on the first day of the tournament, I was sitting on the first tee and Ben Crenshaw, who had just won the Masters, came straight over and started talking to me. I was watching Arnold Palmer and Ben plopped himself down next to me and said, 'You're watching the man himself to get the atmosphere.'

Like an overawed schoolboy, all I could think of to say was, 'Can I have your autograph?'

That was the first time I'd met Ben, and to this day he remembers my first name even though I can't remember ever telling him it. Meeting him was my first recollection of the Open, and the other great moment of 1984 was playing the Road Hole, the famous seventeenth, which Brian was the first to birdie that year. (Later Seve was to play a six iron here into the heart of the green and then see his closest rival Tom Watson – going for a record sixth Open – over- shoot on to the road.) As he was virtually a local, of course, the crowd went wild for Brian; it was my first experience of a large number of people reacting like this – whistling, shouting, clapping, cheering – and it really gave me a great buzz. Brian missed the cut that year but to birdie one of the most famous and difficult holes in golf was a tremendous achievement.

After that I recall running round and collecting the names in the front of my yardage book: Jack Nicklaus, Hale Irwin, Ben and even Seve, whom I approached on the putting green.

The 1988 Open was at Royal Lytham St Annes where Seve had become the youngest winner for almost a century back in 1979. Lytham is a very tough links course, although it's set back off the sea. It's a thinking man's course because position off the tee is so impor- tant, and if the wind gets up the back nine can be very difficult.

I was due to meet Seve on the Sunday of Open week at the house where he was staying in the town. (I had digs fixed up about fifteen minutes away, well out of the way where no one could bother me.) As soon as I arrived he told me to get the clubs in the car as we were going straight out to practise. I liked his attitude. In the two weeks up to the Open his long irons had been going great and he was confident and striking the ball well. He was relaxed and that was another good sign. Personally I was quietly confident because I had also had a premonition that we were going to win. I had this sense that fate was on our side, that this was going to be it.

That Sunday also gave me an insight into the amount of support Seve has in Britain. We went out and played nine holes, four going out and five coming in, just to get the feel of the place again, but there must have been two or three hundred people trailing round with us. All the time people were shouting, 'Come on, Seve! Come on!' and most of them were British. In between holes he signed autographs – another good pointer as to how relaxed he was – while I did my best to take notes, checking the markers, pacing off distances, trying to do my bit in the campaign.

The real work began on the Monday when we worked out the target areas for each hole. Seve would say, 'I don't want to be past this bunker,' or 'That's our target area there,' and down it would go in my book. Nine times out of ten a top pro like Seve will land in his designated target area, as long as you pick the right club. The thing is not to get into trouble, and that's why you set the target areas to approach the green from the right angle and at the same time avoid hazards like bunkers or water. Then again, you'll have a different strategy for different weather. The wind might change, so you'll have contingency plans for wind behind or wind against. The aim is to cut out as much of the element of chance as you can. When play began in the 117th Open Championship, I felt we'd done as much as was humanly possible to pave the road to victory.

On the morning of any big tournament I like to go into my tried-and-tested routine: early rise, breakfast, and down to the course nice and early with the bag ready packed. I organize things so that I'm not rushed into anything, because if you get hassled you might start missing things. I like to go at my own pace. I always check the contents of the bag, which should include two yardage books (one is a spare in case the first goes missing), pencils, pencil sharpeners, a penknife, spare ball markers, some spare Titleist balls (plus one or two in my pocket as well), towels, spare gloves, plasters, nail scissors, two sets of waterproofs and the bag cover in case it rains. I also carry some water and of course fruit (bananas, pears and apples) and a couple of muesli bars in case the energy begins to flag a little. It all fits and the bag balances at around 43 lb. Like most pros Seve likes his clubs in order and I'd learned by the 1988 Open that the putter and the driver, his key clubs, always get the tender-loving-care treatment. The caddie has to be prepared for every eventuality, anything that may arise – a cut finger, a blister, a howling gale. On wet days one of the biggest problems can be keeping the grips dry, because when you stand the bag upright, water comes through the air holes in the bottom. Occasionally with a new bag the strap will squeak a bit, so it has to be broken in before the big day. It's the small details that can win or lose you a tournament.

We were off at 9.25 on the morning of the Thursday of the 1988 Open, and after an hour of practice Seve proceeded to take the course apart with a birdie, birdie, birdie start – two clear of the field – and all my wildest dreams were coming true. I was walking along in a daze and I had to make a real effort to get a grip on myself and start concentrating.

On the fourteenth came trouble, but another clear indication that this was going to be Seve's year. We had a bad lie after the drive and the semi-rough caught the iron and the ball shot off left into a jungle of heather and gorse. It was unplayable and we had to decide where to take the penalty drop. But Seve was thinking ahead. He went back towards the sixth tee, dropped there and I gave him the yardage from there into the green. He hit a good seven iron over the trees to 15 feet, sank the putt and we'd made one of the greatest bogey fives I'd ever seen, as good as a birdie. It had all taken close to half an hour.

He looked at me and I looked at him and we had a smile. That was when I knew for sure that Seve was on his way to a third Open.

The question was: would I be there at the finish with him, because my Open nearly came to an end there and then thanks to skirmish with a very pig-headed spectator. What had happened was that while we were sorting out a line for the drop I had shooed some straying spectators out of the way, but there was one obstinate one who wouldn't budge. He insisted on standing over the ball and trying to get one last look before the shot. I spoke loudly to him and told him to get out of the way in no uncertain terms when he turned really aggressively, got hold of my bag and twisted it almost off my shoulder. I felt a twinge and knew I'd pulled something. After I'd put the gear away that night I was suffering, so I hurried back to my accommodation and had a good long soak. It didn't stiffen up much overnight, but as it was my right, bag-carrying side, I could feel it every time I bent down to pick up the bag. Needless to say, I said nothing to Seve: he had enough on his mind.

One thing we'd planned above everything else was to stay out of the sand, because the bunkers at Lytham are killers. On the second day, however, with a two-shot lead at the start, I got a ticking off because we brought the bunker into play on the third. Fortunately it didn't spoil what was a steadyish round of 71, and we finished the day a shot behind Nick Price.

Then the weather took a hand. The wind had really

freshened towards the end of Friday by the time we were finishing the round, and there were a few squalls getting up, though this was just the start of the deluge. Bright and early on the Saturday I went out to check the pin positions and I knew straight away we were going to struggle to play at all that day. There had been a tremendous amount of rain overnight and it was still throwing it down on the Saturday morning.

'Any chance?' I asked the greenkeeper on the way out, and he replied, 'It doesn't look too good. I think it will be called off today, Ian.'

Back at the clubhouse I called Seve with the news: 'I think we can forget it today – we're not going to get started. Stay there and I'll keep in touch. If we get any sign of a start, I'll ring you back right away, but don't bet on it!'

When I returned to the course, people were splodging about with bales of straw and there was a lot of work going on, but it was in a desperate state and I knew this was going to be another big test for both of us because it was the sort of day where you could get destroyed by boredom. Just after lunch Seve appeared to hit a few balls and stroke a few putts, and happily he seemed very relaxed. He had managed to turn off and was taking the delay in his stride, which was a relief. In many ways, with a good forecast for Sunday, the weather had done us a favour, because the course was playing longer than ever.

On the third day we drew Price and big Craig Stadler and the sort-out began. At Lytham the back nine is what makes or breaks a round because that's where most of the difficulties lie, but you can't do anything about bad luck. On the sixth Seve hit a spectator and the ball rebounded into some bushes behind the ropes. After a bit of a search we found it stuck down in the undergrowth. Looking round we saw that there was no place for a drop even and it was clear to us both that he would have to play it out back-handed. Seve took the eight iron out of the bag and started to try a few practice swings. I was standing slightly behind, 5 or 6 yards away, ready to dive in with another club if he wanted to change the eight, when he looked up and said, 'Move back a bit, Ian.' I drifted back about 10 yards and then he took a swing at the ball and duffed it completely. It hardly moved. I sensed a crisis – even more so when he bawled me out in no uncertain terms because he felt I was getting too close and in the firing line if the ball came out at a funny angle. But finally he played a really good back-hander out on to the fairway. The hole cost a six and I stole a glance back for his reaction. There was a deep breath from Seve but no problems – a birdie on the par five seventh got the momentum going again. A straightforward par on the plateau green of the eighth where Price took a five and another par at nine.

One behind Price, Seve showed how relaxed he was by approaching a policeman with a walkie-talkie to ask how the cricket was going: a good sign!

All week the fourteenth had become the bogey hole for us with an average of around four and three quar-ters for the tournament, and I had to admit I had begun thinking about it long before we got there, which is bad news because you should have everything tuned into the hole in hand. By now Nick Faldo had appeared on the leader board and I knew then that the fourteenth was going to be crucial. It's actually a pretty straightforward par four, but it's into the prevail-ing breeze and you have to get a good drive away because it is a bit tight. On the right there are humps and long grass and on the left there are hollows and long grass, but you can't afford an iron off the tee as you don't want a long iron second into the wind. I knew it was time for a bit of caddie psychology and a bit of subtle encouragement, so I just said, 'Nice easy swing, Seve,' and sure enough he played a good drive down on to the fairway, drifted an iron in right of the hole and we just missed the birdie. Phew, thank God for that – a par!

The fifteenth is tough, too, 468 yards across the wind, but another good drive set us up for a par and it was all going nice and steady. We weren't firing on all cylinders but doing similarly to Price, who was parring everything and looking a big danger – Stadler was out of it; he had a nightmare. There was another birdie chance on the shortish par four sixteenth but the putt just missed, and then it was par, par on the seventeenth and eighteenth to leave us two adrift of Price for the last day.

Monday was a great day for a lot of people, but fortunately the fireworks came mainly from Seve Ballesteros with one of the most spectacular rounds of golf to win a championship ever played. As is his custom, he had his last-day outfit on – all navy blue – and we went out with the Nicks, Price and Faldo. Before long players were throwing eagles and birdies all over the place. Now Seve doesn't like me looking at the scoreboard on the way round, but I do anyway because there might come a point when I could say, 'Let's make sure of making a birdie here,' and I could see Fred Couples and Sandy Lyle creeping up the leader board. Seve had some early birdie chances which he missed but there were no blow-ups; just a little 'I really thought that would break more' and then on with the job.

On the sixth the tournament really took off and

within a short time the Open Championship was down to a two-horse race. The sixth was downwind and slightly left to right and we picked a six iron for the second which he hit to 8 feet for a birdie. We were one shot behind Price and it was so very important to get away a good drive on the seventh, to make every hole going out count, because I knew that, with the wind, it was going to be tricky coming home. Price stuck his second into eagle country, but then Seve hit a beauty straight down the flag all the way. We heard the crowd cheering and I reflected again on just how popular Seve was over here, like an adopted citizen and certainly more popular than Nick Faldo! With Seve on song, the gallery just seemed to flow with him.

Seve's eagle there and Price's eagle put the both of them two shots clear as we turned back into the wind, and I knew it was going to be hard for anyone to come back at us. An uphill birdie putt on the eighth dropped for us and all of a sudden it was head to head with Price.

On the eleventh Seve checked the wind and then punched one in, rolled in a great putt, and we were ahead of Price for the first time. The South African was still looking positive, however, and I thought, 'He's not going to crack easily.'

But then, on the short twelfth, came near-disaster. As they putted out the eleventh I'd picked the bag up and gone off to the next tee to try to assess the wind. I walked to where the trees ran out in the gap and judged that the breeze was coming from left to right. Then I returned to the tee where Seve was waiting, we had a long discussion and eventually I pulled what was to become the famous four iron out of the bag, expecting him to hit his normal left-to-right shot low into the green. But horror of horrors – he hit it straight up in the air and it was never getting there!

Now Seve may be Spanish but he also knows some old-fashioned English and he gave me a right mouthful. This was the real crisis of the week, because we simply couldn't afford him to lose his cool, so I tried to ignore the explosion. I got an instant dose of what I like to call 'the Caddie Syndrome' – deafness in the ear on Seve's side – and just stood there and took it to let him burn out his fuse. I knew that if I answered back, the firework was going to blow up again. Walking down off the tee, I said, 'Come on, let's get it up and down and make three.' He calmed down a bit, but the worst thing was that having gone one shot up we'd given the momentum back to Price with a four on a par three, because Seve's putt for par dived across at the last minute and Nick stuck in a 2-footer to get back level.

As we walked off to the thirteenth Seve muttered, 'Stupid, that, wasn't it?'

'Yes,' I said. 'Come on, let's get on with the next hole.' And he was fine again.

On the thirteenth Nick Price hit probably his best shot of the week to within a couple of inches and Seve had left a 12-footer just to stay on terms. Then all of a sudden I received a real shock when, as Seve started stalking the putt, he suddenly called me over and asked me to read it with him, which was something he hadn't done all week. The teamwork must have succeeded, because he hit in a lovely putt.

'Great putt there, let's keep it going,' a nod of assent and it was on to the fourteenth. Again I knew a four here and a four on the very long fifteenth would do us on the two toughest holes going in.

Nick hit it down the middle but Seve pushed his out right. His second hit a clump of grass and kicked left, yet I wasn't too bothered as we weren't far from the green and I knew from a position like that he could get it dead. But then, after I'd given him a sand wedge for the chip, he changed it to a pitching wedge, hit it too well and it ran on. The putt stayed out and that was another dropped shot on the dreaded fourteenth, but then Nick showed the first sign of the jitters by missing an easy putt way left: a good break for Seve.

By now I'd stopped looking at the board because it just wasn't necessary. It was down to two men and although Nick was playing well I thought my man was better equipped to handle the pressure. The fifteenth has been the graveyard of many Open Championship hopes, including those of the great Jack Nicklaus, but it wasn't to be for Seve that year. Again he pushed his drive out right but we got on in two and his putt – which rolled over Faldo's marker and made it jump in the air – went stone dead for a cast-iron four. Price's putt struggled in and it was there I thought I saw the first flaw, the chink in his putting, and while I sensed that our opponent was feeling the pressure, Seve seemed to be getting stronger and stronger.

On to the sixteenth and a drive over a line of sand-hills to a hidden fairway, a long discussion over whether to take a nine iron or a pitching wedge to the narrow green, then a check on the wind and finally an absolute blinder that spun round the hole and left a tap-in for a birdie. One of the cameramen down by the side of the fairway came up and asked what we'd taken, but I got a look from Seve to say, 'Get up here with me, never mind him.' A little tap in and a smile at the camera, and when Nick made a mess of his birdie putt I thought, 'We've got him!'

Two holes to go, two pars would do it. A perfect drive down seventeen and all the pressure was on Nick again. He responded by almost going out of bounds, getting a drop off some lorry tracks and then playing a brilliant one iron straight on to the green.

Another long talk with Seve on whether to take a four or a five and then he put the five high on to the green inside Price. Both putted up stone dead . . . one to play and one in front – 'Please, God, give us a four!'

The eighteenth was pure agony because we hadn't played it well all week. The drive has to be straight and long to get over the line of bunkers across the middle and there's more waiting out on the left. This time he went out right and I couldn't tell whether he'd caught the sand or if it had trickled past into the semi. My heart was in my mouth as I waited for someone, anyone, to signal that it had gone past the bunker.

Seve was just as anxious and I was waiting for the question. 'Is it in the bunker, Ian?

I took the plunge. 'No, it's past the bunker.'

But all the way down I was trembling because I wasn't sure until finally I saw the crowd milling round a spot on the far side of the trap and I knew we were safe. Or were we?

He had a nice lie and the plan was to hit it left and fade it into the wind, but what should have been a nice, normal six took a shooter and the ball ran off into a little hollow on a downslope in the rough at the back of the green. As we walked up past the cheering masses I pulled my visor down to hide the tears. It was an unbelievably emotional moment but I knew that we weren't on a lap of honour just yet, particularly when I saw what a nasty lie we'd been landed with. Nick was over on the left side of the green a long way away and Seve then produced an unbelievable shot under pressure. Even when I play it back on video now I can still almost convince myself that it's not going in. It was just the greatest shot you could wish to see to win a tournament: the lie wasn't good and to play the shot with such control, precision and pace was just out of this world. To me there was only one person who could have played that shot.

But then that had been Seve all week. When he'd won at Lytham in 1979 he'd spent most of the last round playing out of the car parks round the course and in the seventy-two holes had been in sand fifteen times. This was a different sort of Seve, from beginning to end the man in charge, with everything under control.

Poor Nick charged the hole and as soon as he hit it I knew it was all over because he wasn't even on the right line. Then he missed coming back and I wished at the time he had holed it, as he deserved to. From that moment on I hadn't a clue what was going on. I shook hands with Andy Prodger, Faldo's caddie, and Dave McNeilly, who was carrying Price's bags, then Seve came over and we cuddled in the middle of the green.

'Give me the card,' he said. All he wanted to do was get it signed and out of the way, but I was in tears and wouldn't let go. Finally he got the card off me and I got the putter and ball off him. Someone dragged me off for a radio interview, yet I couldn't say to this day what I babbled on about. Channel Nine TV from Australia shoved a microphone in front of me, then the Press collared me. From the grandstand there appeared a bottle of champagne which I managed to pluck one-handed out of the air, and all around it was bedlam. People were shouting, 'Give us this' or 'Give us that.' The overalls went to a policeman who auctioned them for charity – sorry about that, Royal and Ancient – but

I kept Seve's glove and ball out of the way in my back pocket.

Finally, I pushed and shoved my way into the relative quiet of the locker room. 'Barry the Judge' was there with Andy and Dave and all of a sudden the knees went wobbly, I sat down and burst out crying. I cried like a baby for five minutes, just overcome by the emotion of the moment, the adrenalin and the pure happiness. We opened the champagne and had a drink with the two locker room attendants and the security man, and then the man on the front desk went off and got two more bottles and some ice and we were having our own little party when Nick Price came in. He had played brilliantly but still lost and I couldn't help feeling sick for him.

I said, 'Will you have a drink with us, Nick?'

'More than glad to, Ian,' he replied, which to me showed what class he had, because at that moment he must have felt terrible. He had been beaten again in a Major after seemingly having it won.

I tried to console him. 'Don't you ever think you lost that – it was Seve that won it.'

Then he congratulated me on the job I'd done, which was a tremendous thing for him to say.

At this point a message came from Seve saying he wanted his clubs taken to the car so that he could avoid the crowds. I grabbed the clubs, packed everything in the bag and met him at the car, shook hands and off he went. It was only after he'd gone that I thought, 'Crikey, I've got to get home somehow now!' But then big Geoff Clarke, who was with Tyne Tees Television at the time, came up and asked me to go on TV-am next day, offering to drive me up to Manchester. Without thinking I agreed. I walked slowly back past the empty stands, packed up what gear I had left, said goodbye to everyone and set off home in the car.

Life would never be the same again, as I was to find out in the next twenty-four hours. At the motorway services I had a cup of tea and a sandwich and heard some people whispering, 'That's Seve's caddie.' Fame at last! I got home to Redcar at midnight to find everyone sitting up waiting. Lesley couldn't bring herself to watch us on TV, she told me, then she broke the news that the TV people were picking me up at 4.30 the next morning to drive me up to Manchester. So it was up to the studios, then back home to find the phone ringing non-stop. I could understand Seve being the centre of Press attention, but the papers all wanted my side of the story too – all of them, that is, except my local paper, the *Evening Gazette*, which never even got in touch!

I realized at this point that I was about to find out what it really meant to work for someone like Seve and I realized, too, the responsibility it placed on me. From then on everything I did or said could reflect on him.

It was also the beginning of the end of my financial troubles. That year I cleared up all the debts and started to plan buying the first house that Lesley and I had owned in eighteen years of marriage.

The winning wasn't to stop there, but one man would make sure I kept my feet on the ground. I recalled Seve's last words when we shook hands at Lytham as he climbed into his car.

'Thanks for everything, see you on Tuesday,' he had said.

And I couldn't even remember where we were supposed to be on Tuesday!

7

Every One a Winner

Slowly, as the 1988 season wore on, I got to know a bit more about my employer. I found that we had a mutual interest in soccer. He supported his local team in Santander; I had been a lifelong Middlesbrough fan, and I managed to get him interested in the doings at Ayresome Park. If we were abroad, I'd be looking for the Boro results in the paper while he would be searching to see how Santander went on, and I have been known to bash the odd club into the ground when certain results have been handed to me, particularly if we'd been beaten by Newcastle, the old enemy. When I was at home, the then manager, Bruce Rioch, would always arrange tickets for matches. I'd been in the dressing rooms and met the players and even had my photograph taken with them showing how not to kick a soccer ball. Boro and their struggles to stay in Division One became a major topic of conversation between Seve and me in our moments of relaxation off the course and I'm sure Seve could still reel off that Boro team even now!

Seve's other great interest is cycling, although personally I'd rather he stayed well clear of bikes. We would occasionally have bets on top races like the Tour de France, with him backing Pedro Delgado and me picking Sean Kelly. The year I picked Kelly, of course, he fell off, while Delgado went and won the race, so it was one up to Seve there. If he gets the chance, he will try to take in one or two stages of the Tour and does a lot of cycling himself, giving me a few heart tremors at times. Just before the Suntory in 1988, for instance, he was having a race with some friends when the gear slipped and he shot forward, overbalanced and fell off. Much to my horror he was severely bruised down his arm, elbow and leg, and in fact was lucky he hadn't broken anything. I quietly advised him that it would be better to stay off his bike near tournament times, otherwise my future good fortunes might suffer!

Off the course Seve is as relaxed as the next man and likes nothing better than a good gossip about sport, any sport. In the USA we'd go to basketball matches together, because Seve would often find himself with spare tickets for this or that event. In Florida we went to see the Miami Heat, which is supposed to be the worst team in America, but at the two matches I saw they played out of their skins, leaving me with a 2–0 record, so I'm sure I'll be in big demand whenever I go back there. In taking me to these matches Seve was really just showing consideration for me: he probably realized that I need a break from routine as much as anyone. If I was away somewhere on my own, it wouldn't do me much good simply to stare at four walls in a motel room all evening, so it was nice to get out with him and relax – as much as it was possible to relax in his company, for he was always in the public eye.

On the circuit one of Seve's best mates is Sandy
Lyle and they often go out dining together; and during
the time I was with him I became almost immune to
the sight of celebrities turning up to shake Seve's hand
– people like Nigel Mansell, Tomba, the ski slalom
racer, and TV personalities such as Bruce Forsyth and
Ronnie Corbett. It's great to meet people like this, of
course, but I always had to remember that I was there
to do a job and couldn't just wander round star gazing.

Off the course we could unwind, but as soon as the
gun went I saw a different Seve – a man with the
fiercest will to win and a man who wouldn't tolerate
any slap-happiness. I learned to spot the signs when a
blow-up was on its way. There were the little things you
could recognize and read, such as a couple of bad shots
in a row or a bad bounce. It's amazing how many
times you'll hit what looks the perfect shot and the ball
will kick left when it's supposed to go right or straight.
Eventually things like that would begin to get to him
and I'd see the steam starting to rise. It was then that
you had to step in and encourage him, offering little
carrots like, 'Don't worry, it will come back our way
eventually,' and it always did; it would even itself out,
and he knew that as well as anyone. It just helped him
from time to time to open the steam valves and let fly.
At times like that you just had to switch off and take
it, carefully choosing the time to move back in and
calm him down.

Before our last season together, when I tended to
take a lot of stick for nothing, I think there were two
notable occasions when I really deserved a rocket. One
was the four iron in the British Open of 1988 and the
other was our fairly forgettable performance in the
1989 US Open at Oak Hill, New York, where we
finished tied forty-third. I got very lackadaisical and

the concentration wasn't what it should have been. Perhaps I was extra tired that day, but I wasn't keeping up with Seve and I got thoroughly deserved roasting.

But, then again, Seve showed what a genuine person he was the next day. We went out and had a really good round, and at the end as I went to put the clubs away he said, 'Well done, Ian. There were two clubs you pulled there which helped turn the round around.' So although he was willing to jump on me for doing something wrong, he was just as quick to give me a pat on the back if I'd had a good day. When he'd start screaming I could accept it as long as I knew what he was saying was true, and I had to learn to take it because it was part of my job. And often, even if I didn't really deserve being shouted at, I'd rationalize that most of it was emotion, the Latin temperament stirred up by the experience of a bad day.

At times I could look back on days when I'd done nothing wrong and think, 'You did well today, Ian.' In many ways I've played the perfect round like Seve and I've sat back at night and reflected on a job well done. Perhaps he's picked out a six iron for his shot into the green and I've changed it to a seven and he's hit it next to the pin and tapped it in for a birdie. After that has happened a couple of times a round you really feel you've contributed to the day and that's what really makes the job worthwhile. You may not have won the tournament but you get a sense of: 'That was down to me at the end of the day.'

Sometimes the job satisfaction doesn't just come from club selection or picking the right line on a green. At the Dutch Open once I went out without the bag cover and both sets of waterproofs and it was pouring, yet I still managed to keep the clubs and the grips dry when strictly speaking they should have been wringing wet. That could have turned into a real disaster.

There was another near-miss in the Lancôme Trophy at St Nom la Breteche, close to Versailles, in 1988. The fifteenth is a dog leg to the left with a plateau or two. Coming towards the ball down the hill, I reached for the yardage book to do my usual checks. Normally I carry the bag on the right with the book in the back left trouser pocket, but when I reached down for it there was nothing there. Now at that point I was reasonably calm, thinking that I'd just stuck it in another pocket, but I went through all my pockets, through the bag, and there was no sign of it.

I plucked up courage and told Seve, 'I think I've lost the yardage book.'

'It must be in your pocket. Have another look.'

After another more frantic search there was still no book. I remembered having it in my hand at the tee, so I took off like Linford Christie 250 yards back up the hill full tilt. But the book wasn't at the tee. In the meantime – unknown to me – Seve had gone across to Jose-Maria Olazabal to get the yardage for the shot and was standing there waiting when I came belting back. By now I was in an absolute panic – and this was the caddie who was supposed to be Mr Cool – but then a French official prodded me in the backside and sure enough there was the book in the right back trouser pocket.

'I've found the yardage book,' I told Seve, somewhat shamefaced.

'You dozy so and so,' he said, but fortunately he saw the funny side of it. 'That's another first for me be-cause I've never had a caddie who's lost the book before.' And then he continued talking in Spanish to

Olazabal and they both had a good laugh at my expense. I must have had a complete brainstorm that day – fortunately it wasn't a Major – because I had also forgotten the spare yardage book which was in the bag all the time!

Still I was reasonably pleased with the way the teamwork was coming along, although I have to admit I never felt on the same wavelength as Seve where shot-making was concerned. Some of his stroke-making was beyond your wildest dreams. Two shots in particular stand out in our first year together, both in the Suntory World Matchplay at Wentworth against the same man, Mark McCumber, who must have wondered what he had done to deserve such treatment twice in a day.

We were on the 399 yard par four seventh and playing into a howling gale blowing from left to right. Seve laid his drive out to the right in just about the worst position you could find, on a downslope, behind a big tree and in a valley with a plateau green to reach for the second. The only shots I could visualize were either to pitch back out and try to get close with a third or to punch a seven iron low over the brook that ran across below the green. I got ready with one or two suggestions, but Seve just took a one iron out of the bag. He had obviously seen something in his own mind no one else could see, and at times like that, even though I hadn't a clue, I just let him get on with it. He cut this one iron round the tree into the wind and finished pin high on the edge of the green. It was just incredible; I couldn't even have imagined a shot like that.

Then, after we had finished all square with McCumber, it was back down the first for sudden death. Seve played the shot that finished the contest, a three wood into the wind that was the most perfect strike, covering the flag all the way – sheer genius under pressure.

After the triumph of Lytham things slowly got back to normal for me. The phone calls died down and by then I had worked out where we were to be the following Tuesday ... in Drottingholm, Sweden, for the Scandinavian Enterprise Open, and the dream continued when Seve was victorious with a good, solid display over the week, winning by five clear shots in what were almost anti-climactic rounds of 67–70–66–67.

It was a good warm-up for the US PGA, my first trip to America, where I had arranged to stay with the grandparents of Jamie Howell, the young American pro who got his player's card back that year. Just to reverse the coin, we experienced our first missed cut, although as it turned out it could have been a lot more serious. During this trip I first came across the perennial problem of playing abroad in an unfamiliar climate and endured my first insight into how heat and humidity can play a huge part in your performance. Every day I was pouring sweat in temperatures of 95–100°F and there was no relief anywhere.

In the second round of the tournament Seve came close to a really nasty accident when his tee shot on sixteen landed on the baked green as if it were a road and bounced through the back of the green into a clump of grass close up to the wall that went all the way round. Seve tried to play it out but bladed the ball badly and it ricocheted off the wall like a bullet and just missed his head. It came off the wall at such a pace that it could almost have killed him had it made contact. We had to make do with a double bogey there that put us out of it. Again, it was part of the learning process for me. I should have made him take a drop, made sure of a four and tried for a couple of birdies on the next couple of holes. As it was, the incident unsettled him a bit.

After two wins on the trot it was a bit of a rude awakening to go all that way out there, paying my own fare and missing the cut; it showed me more than ever what a fine line there was between being successful and failing to break even. But we were back on the streak at the German Open in Frankfurt where Seve achieved his third win that year and I got a £2,000 wristwatch – courtesy of my boss!

The organizers had put up the Rolex as a prize for the lowest round, and on the last day Seve was tearing the course apart. We had a three-shot lead going into the last and it was just a case of playing out, collecting the cheque and heading home. We'd played our second and were walking on to the green and Seve was starting to look up and down the line of the putt when Denis Durnian, our playing partner, turned to me and said, 'You'd better go and tell Seve he's got this putt for the Rolex for the lowest round.'

He had the putt for a 63 but I said to Dennis, 'I can't tell him that now.'

'Go on, go and tell him – it will make him concentrate better.'

So when I walked on to the green to clean the ball, I said to Seve, 'You've got this putt for the watch for the lowest round.'

He looked at me slyly and replied, 'Don't you think I know that? I tell you what, Ian, come and read this putt and if I hole it the watch is yours.'

The whole crowd heard this and I thought, 'Well, we're in trouble now, because there's not a chance of getting this right.'

I read it as a ball outside the right of the hole and I

was tending the flag when Seve set the ball off at least 3 inches outside my line. Then it all seemed to happen in slow motion, as if the ball were travelling through wet concrete, but about 2 yards away it kicked off a spike mark, then took another kick left, caught the back of the hole, ran round it and finally dropped in.

I don't think anyone has seen two bigger smiles in your life, but I still thought it was odds against my getting the watch. I went back to the locker room to start packing and bought the six or seven caddies there a beer. We were waiting to set off to Switzerland for the next tournament when someone walked in and said, 'Seve's just announced it in public – he's giving the watch to his caddie!' Ten minutes later, after all the speeches and prize-giving, Seve walked in – with the watch on his wrist.

'This watch looks a lot nicer than my watch,' he said. 'I think I should keep it.'

But then he broke out into a big grin, took it off his wrist and handed it over while all the caddies gave a big cheer.

My main problem on the way home was customs. Seve's gesture was all over the papers by this time, so I just did the honest thing and walked through the red channel, paid up and finished up with a clear conscience.

At Crans we were in contention to win again with four to go, but then two duffed chips and a putt which finished balanced on the hole at the last cost us that. However, a second wasn't to be complained about and my debts at home were being reduced all the time, although Seve himself managed to cut my incomings by £5 at the next tournament, the Lancôme. Again he was cruising to victory on the last day . . . five or six shots clear and he was just going through the motions.

He dropped a couple of shots on the way out in a very lackadaisical way and, just to liven things up a bit, I bet him a fiver that he couldn't pull back to par for the round. At this he got a gleam in his eye and started to play as if the Open were at stake until, on the last, he needed a birdie to get back to level. In went the putt on eighteen and Seve walked straight over and demanded the fiver – he wasn't worried about the tournament. 'A bet's a bet,' he said, and he wanted his winnings!

With one Major and three other tournament wins, we hadn't had a bad start to our relationship, but the streak had to end somewhere. After beating Mc-Cumber at the first extra hole at Wentworth, Sandy Lyle gave us a real drubbing in the semi-final, 7 and 6 with Sandy sinking his putts and Seve missing most of his. Then the Australians beat Spain in the semi-finals of the Dunhill Cup, Greg Norman shooting 67 to our 69, and finally there was a good second place in the Volvo Masters when Nick Faldo shot a last-round 68 to snatch victory.

My whole life had been transformed by the few months with Seve. We were back in the black at home and I was finally able to do what I'd promised Lesley for so long: walk into a building society for a mortgage and buy our own home. When they asked my profession I said, 'Golf caddie,' which caused a stir, but I showed them my accounts and they accepted my application. We moved over to Kirkleatham Lane, still in Redcar but a little nearer the golf club and the working men's club. It meant a great deal to Lesley and a great deal to me too. We had no thought of leaving sunny Redcar, of course. Mum and Dad still live there about a mile and a half away and my brother Keith is just 800 yards down the road.

By now Mark, my elder son, was in the RAF and although Damon was still at school he had already started to caddie occasionally. Mark has never really been interested in sport and I think he used to get a bit fed up with his mates saying, 'There's your Dad on telly,' but underneath I think he felt proud too. Damon, on the other hand, was the first to go round saying, 'My Dad's caddying for Seve.'

Damon's a keen golfer down at the Cleveland club and occasionally I would try to fit in a round there in the winter – it never closes. Funnily enough, my game started improving after I began working with Seve, even though I had no time to practise. Occasionally I would address the ball and think, 'How would Seve do it? Perhaps I'll try and fade it on to the green,' and of course I'd finish up bumping it on the floor. Down at the golf club and the working men's club they kept my feet firmly on the ground and there was no chance to be big-headed. Despite all the attention from the TV and Press and public I tried to stay the same, although I was always aware that Seve had had confidence and trust in me and that I had to be honest and straightforward and keep the confidences to myself. People were always approaching me to ask questions about life with him and I had to learn to handle that too.

Towards the end of the year I broke new ground for the bag carriers of the world. While Pete Coleman may have been the first caddie with a Porsche, I was the first to have a management company working for me. I thought it might be a good idea because I was finding it a bit hectic trying to organize everything, and I thought that, with the new high profile of caddies, the company might be able to land me a few contracts. But as it turned out, while they had a few footballers among their clientele they were completely clueless about golf and golfers and in the end it cost me money. For example, they would always arrange the most expensive travel, whereas I just wanted – as in the past – the most sensible prices. A trip that might normally cost, say, £1,200 would come to £1,700. It wasn't practicable, so eventually I got rid of them. As they had Gazza on their books at the time I don't suppose they starved!

So I stayed out of the limelight as much as possible, which was somewhat easier in Redcar, where I was away from everybody and everything, than it would have been in, say, London. Yet there was still quick access from my home to plane flights and thus to the world.

By the time the 1989 season got into full swing my face had become quite familiar down at Teesside Airport, but as I flew out for the first tournament of the year there were a few clouds gathering on the horizon.

8

Master Plan

THE SEASON FOR ANY CADDIE begins with a telephone call to your player or his office to work out where and when he is going to need you that year, and in January 1989 I rang the office of Seve's management company in Santander. I spoke to Joe Collet, the American who looks after the Ballesteros business affairs, who gave me a rough schedule for the year so that I could begin making plans. Then I spoke to Seve who announced that he was feeling good and fit and raring to go. For me, winter meant keeping a semblance of fitness, ready for what I call the walking-in period of the first two or three weeks back at work.

Seve had decided to begin in America that year to give himself a good run-in to the US Masters in April. He has his favourite places to play, invariably somewhere he can feel some sun on his back early in the season. We began at the Doral Ryder Open in Miami in February, where he played steady for a top twenty finish, but then came the illness which was to ruin our season in many ways because he never really got over

79

it. We were at Eagle Trace, Coral Springs, for the Honda Classic and he contracted a virus. He looked pretty awful when we played the Pro Am but shot a 64, which in retrospect was a bad thing because it encouraged him to play the tournament when he would have been better off resting. On the Wednesday night before the tournament he had a temperature of 104° and was sweating heavily, so he went to hospital for a check-up. Somehow he got out for the start but he shot a 77, five over, and then after nine holes on the Friday retired. I knew at this point that he must have felt bad, because the last thing Seve wants to do is let people down.

Still, a week later, he was out again, shooting 71 and 74 on the first two days of the Baleares Open in Majorca, then subsiding to a 79 – our worst score together – and a final 71.

Down at the local bookies I still got 7–1 on Seve to win the Masters and in mid-March we flew out to the States once more to begin the final preparations, starting with the New Orleans Open and then the Houston Open. I mentioned that Seve likes to get the sun on his back early in the year, but New Orleans had other plans. Seve arrived late because he had lost his clubs and then it rained all day on the Tuesday, and practice day on Wednesday was washed out after one hole. On Thursday we finally got going – starting on the tenth with an even par round. We were level par again on the Friday and a good round on Saturday saw us two under before a final 71, including (unusual for Seve) a missed putt from 6 inches when he tried to backhand it in.

At Houston – where I got a $100 tip in the Pro Am – we finished second in the shoot-out after the organizers decided that Seve and John Mahaffey would chip out of a bunker and the nearest to the flag would win. Typically of our luck, Seve got out to 6 inches and then Mahaffey splashed out to 3!

Although Seve was playing well, there were some worrying errors beginning to creep into his game. He started hooking a lot, especially under pressure, and on the last day, when we were in with a chance of a win, he went out of bounds at fifteen, although I must hold my hands up and take some of the blame. It's a long (530 yards plus) par five and he was on a bit of a roll at the time, having eagled thirteen and birdied fourteen. On fifteen he hit a good drive but the three wood he took for the second went straight out of bounds. The six there cost us the tournament and when we finished he turned round and said, 'You should have given me a driver for that second shot.'

'Why?'

'You saw me hooking all day but the one club I can't hook is a driver and I could have chased it up there comfortably with a driver.'

So I got a bit of a roasting for that and he was dead right. A fourth place wasn't bad, however, and I wasn't too disappointed because I felt his confidence was coming back for the Masters.

Seve had won twice at Augusta in the past – in 1980 and 1983 – and it has always been one of his big targets to make it a hat-trick, because if there is one thing that will get him motivated it is the thought of beating the Americans at anything, particularly if it's on their home ground. It was my first trip to what is rated one of the world's top courses, so I was looking forward to it, although I was to become a bit disillusioned by the end of the week.

For a start I've never known a place with more rules and regulations. The security was incredibly tight and people there were very officious. It meant I couldn't prepare as I had been used to. I couldn't go out and take the measurements – they expected everyone to trust their pin chart – and I couldn't plan the days as I wanted. In the end I just went out and checked them all by eye and if they looked longer I made them longer on the chart: not our usual meticulous preparation.

I stayed at the Knight's Inn with Steve Williams, who was then caddying for Greg Norman and on the Monday Seve arrived for some practice on the paddock and a bit of putting before we set out for a round with Bernhard Langer and Gary Player. To see that course first hand in all its glory was something special. TV doesn't give a true perspective of it; it is far more spectacular and colourful – and difficult – than anyone can picture. The course was immaculate with not a weed in sight and the crowds were out of this world too. Even on practice days they were massive and clapped every player on to the greens, applauded every good shot, hooted and hollered – so different from any other tournament I'd been to. When I first went to America it had come as a bit of a shock to hear all the whistling and shouting, for the natives are a lot louder and more vociferous than European crowds. Most of them are very knowledgeable about the game, although they haven't a clue what Seve's name is. They would keep calling him Stevie: 'Yeah, come on, Stevie, right on!'

For the first two days the weather was perfect and I thought, 'This is going to be marvellous,' but I still had a few lessons to learn. The speed of the greens was incredible. Slick wasn't the word, but what I hadn't realized on the practice days was they had the course set up specifically for practice. A player could hit the ball on to the green, spin it off and then it would hold on the side of the banks. But when the tournament started they had cut the grass the other way and the ball would spin off and run down into the water. So they trick the course up for practice and then trick it back for the tournament: a bit devilish!

After a wet Wednesday with Jerry Pate and Ben Crenshaw playing with us, we finally drove off for Seve's crack at the Masters. He began with a solid 71, which could have been better, but on the thirteenth he tried to play out of water and took six and we finished the day four shots behind the surprise early leader, Lee Trevino. The second day paired us with Jumbo Osaki as the temperature plunged to 50°F, and while we played well up to the fourteenth, four putts on fifteen cost dear and we finished with 72, not too bad when the average for the day was almost 76.

The Saturday, cold and wet, was about as miserable as you could picture, the sort of day when you wished you'd picked some other way of making a living. The umbrellas came up and went down, the waterproofs went on and off again and eventually play was finished early with us groping round in the dark. We were out with Ben Crenshaw, who was starting to play really well, but the organizers called us in on the fourteenth, Seve having lost three shots on the last three holes. It was a demoralizing end to a demoralizing day and there was the worse prospect of getting up early next day to finish the round before starting the final eighteen holes. I felt really down that night, but Seve was once again to astonish with his ability to pick himself up and perform like a true champion.

We went out in a thundering 31 to take a one-shot lead over Mike Reid and Scott Hoch. Nine holes to go and Seve's hat-trick was on the cards: could we do it?

Then, on the tenth, the momentum began to die a little, possibly because of a ten-minute hold-up when Ken Green objected to Seve's getting a drop off some footprints made by the crowd after he had hooked his tee shot. Apparently Green had an earlier decision that went against him and wanted a second opinion, so eventually the umpire appeared . . . and ruled against us. The bogey there took some of the edge off Seve's game: we went par, par, par through eleven, twelve and thirteen before the incident that stopped him getting back into contention.

On fourteen he had a 6-foot putt for birdie which he missed and fifteen was another chance that got away. It's a par five, and after a good drive his two iron went left of the green. But he chipped up to 8 feet and was crouched over the birdie putt when a huge roar came from the sixteenth to greet a Greg Norman birdie. The noise caught Seve on his backswing and he pushed it out right.

Then it was on to sixteen and one of my worst moments in golf. We decided that it was 162 metres to the pin, 157 metres to the centre of the trap that guards the front, so it was a normal six iron for Seve. He hit what looked like a perfect straight shot at the flag, it landed roughly 1–2 yards short of the green and rolled slowly back into the lake. A little to the right and it would have been perfect. It felt like the end of the world as I watched that ball roll into the water. Seve then hit an eight iron to 4 feet, missed the putt back and it was a double bogey.

Standing on the seventeenth tee was one of the worst moments since I'd been caddying for him. He didn't say anything but his face changed and he just looked so very, very sad. It was then I realized how much he had wanted to win the Masters.

The next hole was a real trial, because somehow I had to settle him and get him to make a final effort. I can remember saying, 'Come on, we can still finish in style,' and being the man he is and the champion he is, Seve raised his head and finished par, birdie.

On the eighteenth he made the famous gesture on the birdie putts: 'If only they had dropped.' Then he waved to the crowd and they gave him a fantastic reception as one of the true greats of golf.

He must have been at his lowest ebb, but still he went through his duties, giving a Press conference. I met him on the way back outside the clubhouse and we put our arms round each other and burst out crying. Just seeing his face I couldn't help it. I knew how much effort he had put into that tournament and I had a terrible, terrible feeling of helplessness and hopelessness. I told him, 'It was a magnificent effort,' but it was something you could never forget, and to be honest the feeling stayed with us for the rest of that year.

I walked back to where I was staying and it was the loneliest walk in the world. I replayed in my mind everything that had gone on and I kept thinking about that six iron, telling myself it must have been the wrong club, blaming myself. I saw Steve with Greg Norman who, with Hoch, had had a chance to win too, but had bogeyed the last, so I went out by myself and had a few bevvies. I met an absolutely plastered Andy Prodger who'd won with Faldo and tried to smile and feel happy for him, but all I could think of was that six iron, the ball rolling slowly into the creek and Seve's sad face.

A week later the smile was back on his face and mine – for a time at any rate. We'd gone out to the Real Club de la Puerto de Hierro in Madrid for the

Cepsa Spanish Open. Seve is like a god on his home ground, of course, and that week he played like one, finishing 16 under and a shot clear of Howard Clark and winning a car into the bargain.

At Valencia a week later the hook had developed again and he played very ordinarily for a ninth place. He didn't seem relaxed at all but there was another swing in fortunes at Chepstow where they were holding the Epson Grand Prix of Europe Matchplay, a format that Seve always enjoys as his successes in the Suntory at Wentworth and the Ryder Cup show. Lesley came down with me and it turned into a perfect week with Seve playing some wonderfully consistent golf – I don't think anyone could have lived with him that week. A total of twenty-seven birdies and two eagles in seventy-three holes speaks for itself and no one really got close to him, although Mark Mouland put up a good fight in the quarter-finals, losing by two holes on the eighteenth in the end. We had Denis Durnian in the final but after the first four holes, all of which Seve won, the contest was as good as over. He had the most spectacular start with a drive and a three wood to a few inches for what would have been an albatross and from there on Dennis was on the ropes. All in all, that was probably the finest week of golf I'd had with Seve, but life after that was like living on a roller coaster.

At the Italian Open at Monticello in May I had some bad news from home: Dad had had a stroke. I decided to keep it from Seve and Mum had said to carry on, but obviously my concentration wasn't what it should have been and I think he sensed something was wrong. In the end I told Carmen, his wife, and she told him straight away. Every day after that Seve would ask how my Dad was, which again showed me what sort of a human being he is because he was playing badly and still found time to think of me.

At the PGA at Wentworth he shot 73–74–65–68, which just wasn't the true Seve form. I felt there was a lot of room for improvement but it wouldn't come.

At the US Open at Oakhill he was in a bad mood all week. The weather was awful and they had to pump the course to make it playable. Seve had a last-round 69 to cheer himself up a bit, but I had the feeling this wasn't to be our year as far as the Majors went.

My son Damon came out with me to the French Open at Chantilly to caddie for Keith Waters, which was great for both of us, but Seve was struggling again. Something was definitely wrong with his game – he was hitting everything out left and trying to guard against it. In practice we worked hard to try to pinpoint the problem, yet there was still no consistency. On the Friday he shot a 64 for a course record and the lead, but on Saturday and Sunday he was down in the dumps because nothing would go right again.

It was up at 4.45 am on the Monday for a flight to Monte Carlo and another nightmare. Seve's virus had returned and he went into the tournament without practice and feeling ill. On the first hole of the first round we lost a ball and things just grew worse from then on, finishing with our missing the cut – the first in Europe and not a good omen for the Open at Troon.

It was nice to be back at the Open but this time I was to see the other extreme, sitting in the locker room on the final day watching the leaders go out. From winning it one year to coming virtually last the next was a sobering experience. Practice had gone badly and I wasn't too hopeful by the time Thursday came round. Seve was not a happy man. He said he just didn't know where the ball was going, and after battling to make the cut we finished tied in seventy-sixth place. Walking up the eighteenth again was so different it was untrue, although the crowd were still behind Seve.

After the highs of 1988 I was beginning to find out what the lows were like. I wondered privately if I was going to get the blame for the bad form. Out in Holland for the Dutch Open the following week, I didn't feel like carrying on caddying. It was sad to see Seve struggling, the weather was awful and I made a bad mistake on the first day which put my own morale at rock bottom. On the eleventh, a par three, I gave him a six iron but I read the wind wrong, I got everything wrong and he cleared the green completely. We just made the cut, but at the end of the third round we were both as low as you could get.

In the locker room I said to him, 'If you feel it would help, I'm willing to quit and let someone else have a go.'

He answered, 'Ian, it has never entered my head to change caddies. Now cheer up!'

Of course, that did cheer me up, and the next day, while he had a good round of 67, I also managed to distinguish myself with a bit of caddie improvisation. Seve had gone out to practise under the eye of Vicente Fernandez to see if he could spot anything wrong with his swing and I went to the putting green to see Steve Williams who was carrying for Leif Hederstrom. Among other things we discussed the weather; and Steve was adamant that it was going to stay fine for our round and on that basis I left the waterproofs behind. Half-way down the first, however, the wind got up and the rain arrived – so much for Steve as a weather forecaster. I gave him a mouthful as we stood there getting soaked and then I realized I hadn't seen the bag hood for a time so there was a good chance of getting all the grips wet.

Seve said, 'It must be in the locker room,' so I sent a spectator back to the clubhouse for the hood and the waterproofs and for four or five holes we carried on with the towel over the clubs. Eventually the spectator got back ... with one set of waterproofs and no hood. I gave Seve the trousers, used the jacket to cover the clubs, gritted my teeth and carried on getting soaked!

Then Seve started playing really well in the wind and that cheered us both up as he moved from tied last to eleventh, although we finished bogey, par, bogey, par as the wind got up to gale force. At least I knew my job was safe – for a time at least – but with Ryder Cup selection coming up we were desperate to get another good finish to make sure he'd be selected on merit and be at The Belfry on 22 September. The slump continued for four more tournaments, however. He played some terrible shots and it was awful to see him suffering, disappearing down the field and not knowing where the ball was going.

The final selection for the Ryder Cup was due to be made in the German and Swiss Opens and we had another disaster in Frankfurt, finishing tied thirty-eighth, so it was all down to the Swiss at Crans-sur-Sierre on 31 August and sure enough Seve produced a touch of magic to win it. We'd battled away all week to stay with the leaders and on the last day the main dangers to us were Craig Parry, who'd won the week before in Germany, and a Swiss, Paolo Quirici, who was finishing strongly.

On fifteen we were one ahead, thanks to Parry taking a six, and we then parred sixteen and birdied seventeen. On eighteen we decided on an iron for safety because a par would win it, but Seve blocked it right and the ball finished on a downslope in the trees. he had a good lie and there was a breeze blowing from left to right. With 130 yards to the flag I was thinking, 'Punch a little seven iron in,' when he took a five iron out of the bag. I did not state my thoughts because it was obviously a shot he'd 'seen' himself and which no one else could and he then proceeded to cut this miraculous five iron left to right into the wind and it dropped down pin high left of the flag and with two putts from 10 yards to win the tournament.

So, after all the downs and disappointments of that year, we were back in the winner's enclosure. Yet the downs and ups still continued. You never knew what was going to happen from one ball and one shot to the next. Lesley had been out there for the week and it was now twice that she had been to a tournament and we had won on each occasion, so I was beginning to wonder whether she shouldn't come out full-time on the tour!

I had a week off before the Lancôme Trophy but Steen Tinning, a young Danish player, had asked me to go to Walton Heath and carry for him in the Panasonic European Open – he needed a couple of thousand pounds to guarantee his card. Damon was down there with Keith Waters and I thought, 'Why not?' Seve didn't like me working on what should have been weeks off – he always said I needed the rest as much as he did. But my answer was always the same: if we were winning tournaments and making money, I wouldn't need to work overtime!

Steen shot 71 and 71 in the first two rounds but the wind got up in the third and we made 79. 'Here we go again,' I thought. But on the last day he managed to keep his form and finished with another 71, tied thirty-sixth. It gave him £2,450 and 117th place in the final points order. Unfortunately, Steen's career was interrupted by a serious car crash later and when I caddied for him again – after I'd split with Seve – he was still on the road to recovery.

With the Ryder Cup looming I should have been worried about Seve's inconsistent form but in the back of my mind I knew that when the gauntlet was thrown down he would be the first to pick it up, especially with it being matchplay and against the Americans. He had kept a positive attitude towards it too. He'd say, 'Don't worry about my form, Ian. We'll beat them,' and I began to believe him.

The Ryder Cup would complete my set of major tournaments and it wouldn't disappoint. The three days there provided some of the most enthralling sporting drama ever seen. And Seve was at the heart of it.

9

Viva Europe!

PEOPLE OFTEN ASK ME about my favourite golf
course and my answer is always the same: I don't have
one. I see golf as a business, and although I enjoy
being on courses I treat them as my workplace. One or
two courses, however, hold special memories. Gleneagles is a beautiful place when the weather's fine. I
remember measuring the course out there early one
morning and a deer bolted from cover across the fairway right in front of me. You don't see that too often
in Redcar!

The people up in Scotland are fantastic – very knowledgeable about the game – and to go round somewhere
like St Andrews is a real experience because there is
always the feeling of nostalgia and tradition there. It
has an old world charm about it and when the wind
blows there is a very special challenge for player
and caddie.

Lytham has a particular place in my heart because
of our Open win on that course, and in the same
category must be The Belfry, near Sutton Coldfield,

particularly after the events there in September 1989. The Brabazon at The Belfry was designed by Peter Alliss and Dave Thomas seventeen years ago. When they started work it was just a large potato field with a lake and a stream running through it and it's the water here that gives the course its American-style challenges. It is still a young course and does need to mature, but it is improving all the time and of course the finishing holes are always interesting. The eighteenth, as we were to see, comes into its own when the pressure is on because you have both the drive and the second shot over the water, and the three-tiered green is over 60 yards long, a potential difference of four clubs. It can be a real test of nerve.

The par four tenth at The Belfry is another famous hole, thanks mainly to Seve. It was in 1978, when he was playing for Europe against Britain in the Hennessy Cognac Cup, that he startled his opponent, Nick Faldo – who had just played up short of the water, as was the custom – by pulling out his driver and fading the ball 300 yards on to the green. There's now a plaque on the tee to mark the feat, although several have equalled it since. It's a great hole for the spectators, but it's not really a difficult shot. We normally take a three wood and knock it up high so that the ball drifts over the fir trees, and it's always going to hit the green. However, it is a challenge under pressure with the stream zigzagging up the left side and the bank on the right.

I could never see The Belfry as an Open venue because it couldn't take the crowds. There's a limit of 20,000, and people wouldn't be able to see as much as they wanted because they can only sit at certain holes. It is also too tight a course, and in any case I'm of the school that believes an Open should be played on a links course. But for the Ryder Cup 1989 The Belfry served very well and most players, particularly the Americans, found the test tough enough.

If there is one certain thing to get Seve Ballesteros fired up and on form it's the thought of a Ryder Cup meeting with the Americans. Probably the feeling is mutual. As far as this tournament goes Seve considers himself a European, and over the years he has had a few altercations with a certain American administrator, which means that there is no love lost between them. Seve has had to take a lot of flak over there, mainly because he *is* Seve and the world's number one player – something that certain Americans have found hard to stomach. They have trouble accepting that anyone from outside their country could be the best in the world of golf.

The problem is that Seve tends to carry the can in the USA for all the Europeans. Six or seven of them might be objecting to the number of tournaments they are supposed to play there to gain exemptions, but for some reason it's always Seve who is singled out to throw the bricks at. In his early days there were a lot of sleights, too, real as well as imagined.

So if anyone wants to see Seve wound up and motivated, all they have to do is mention Americans in general or Tom Kite in particular and then watch him go! If ever we needed an incentive to play well, they could just give us Tom Kite to tee off with because Seve would go round firing 150 per cent then! The incident that sparked all this was before my time with Seve, but apparently Kite made some disparaging comments about him which got back to Seve and caused some resentment. Since then, whenever Tom Kite's name comes up, I watch the bristles rise. I'm sure there are some Americans who feel the same about drawing Seve, because he is the biggest challenge of them all. At The Belfry they were almost queuing up to get a crack at him.

When the non-playing captain, Tony Jacklin, announced the European line-up it was very much as expected, although personally I would like to have seen Sandy Lyle there because he has a certain intimidatory air about him and, like Seve, form doesn't mean too much when it comes to matchplay because you can afford the odd bad hole. But Sandy, to his credit, had decided he wasn't playing well enough and asked to be left out – which just about sums him up as a bloke.

The Americans looked very strong on paper, yet I thought they had made an error in omitting Steve Jones. Lanny Wadkins had a good Ryder Cup record but the last time I had seen him in the States he hadn't been playing at all well.

As it was my first Ryder Cup I didn't really know what to expect and it really didn't start too promisingly. I had flown in from the Lancôme Trophy in Versailles on the Sunday before the tournament began because Seve had wanted me there a day early, but I arrived to find that no room had been booked in my name so there was a bit of unwanted hassle getting that sorted out. Then they gave me a room next to an entrance door which would have been banging away all night so I had to change rooms. I don't think I'm the most popular person in the world with that hotel receptionist!

It wasn't a good way to kick things off from the organization point of view and then Seve had problems with plane connections and didn't arrive until late on Monday night, missing the players' reception. But I managed to get out on the course with Andy Prodger to do some measuring and it was in very good condition. It was the first time I had seen it for a while and it was good to note how the trees had grown and how it was beginning to develop. The greens looked in top-notch condition too.

Seve went straight out on the Tuesday to work on his game before Jacklin sent us out to practise in the formation in which we were expected to play, which meant us partnering Jose-Maria Olazabal. You could see that the Europeans were going to need very little motivation for this one and Seve was really keen, going round chatting to everybody, encouraging them, trying to get involved all the time. It was clear that no prisoners would be taken.

The team spirit among the caddies was fantastic too, because we were part of that team. We'd had a bit of hassle over the clothing we were supposed to wear, but after a slight altercation common sense prevailed and the organizers kitted us out with some nice gear. The caddies really appreciated that, particularly those who were there for the first time, because in many ways we were representing our countries like the players.

People who perhaps didn't normally get on too well together all buckled down to the job in hand. The caddies who had a late draw went out and got the pin positions for the ones with an early draw and there was a real feeling of pulling together. Unfortunately, the man who didn't see it that way was the one in whose best interests it was to have the caddies pulling together and that was Tony Jacklin. As far as the caddies were concerned Jacklin was a man of few words. I think I spoke perhaps ten words to him in the whole of the Ryder Cup – and I was caddying for his main striker! I've always found him very aloof, which seems strange in a team event like the Ryder where a good all-round spirit is vital.

My first tournament win as a caddie with local professional David Whelan.

With David Llewellyn another winner.

With Magnus Persson.

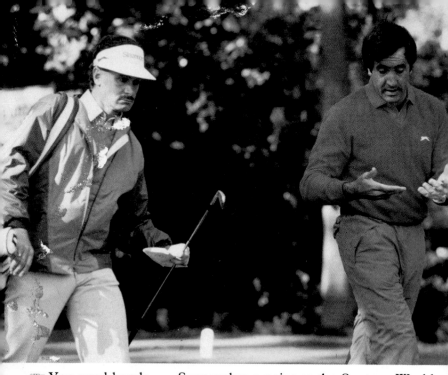

You need hands . . . Seve makes a point at the Suntory World Matchplay in 1988.

Two shots from glory . . . the 72nd hole, Lytham St Annes, in 1988.

On the road to victory . . . Lytham St Annes, 1988.

Some of his shots left me breathless . . . Seve pulls another one out of the bag at the 1988 Suntory.

Rumble in the jungle . . . Seve and I work out the options at the 14th at Lytham.

My favourite outfit
. . . at the Augusta
Masters in 1989.

Ryder Cup 1989 . . .
and referee Andy
McPhee sits this one
out.

Time to celebrate for me, Olazabal and Seve after the Ryder Cup win over Strange and Kite. Curtis looks somewhat disappointed while American captain Ray Floyd hurries over to commiserate.

Birdies galore . . . on the famous 10th hole at the Belfrey with Seve and Jose Maria Olazabal.

Happy days . . . with
'Akeem the Dream'
(7 feet 1 inch) of the
Huston Rockets.

A break in the action
at the 1988 Volvo
Masters.

How not to do it. Ian with Middlesbrough AFC players. *Left to right*: Alan Kernaghan, Tony Mowbray, Gary Pallister (now with Manchester United) and Stuart Ripley.

Bridge over troubled water . . . the 17th at the US PGA, Kemper Lakes, Illinois, and a missed cut just around the corner.

Bernard Gallacher, Jacklin's second-in-command, was a different kettle of fish altogether and I think he will do a great job when he takes over. There was a lot of talk about the captains motivating the players but really when they're in a Ryder Cup they don't need much geeing up – they can do it themselves. People who perhaps don't normally talk to each other for one reason or another will egg each other on, encouraging and cheering.

I know at the end when he was interviewed on TV, Christy O'Connor had some kind words for Seve about the help Seve had been to him. Seve was like that with everyone. I think that at some time in the future he will make a great Ryder Cup captain – he can frighten people into playing for him!

Apart from the caddies and the players, there was also invaluable help from wives and girlfriends. Carmen, Seve's wife, was there – a smashing girl who invariably follows her husband everywhere and gets stuck in in all weathers. If ever we needed a sandwich or some sustenance, Carmen would always oblige. My wife Lesley gets on very well with her and they would often walk the course together.

On the Wednesday and the Thursday of the tournament the players went out and played to the different formats – matchplay, medal, nine holes – trying to get the pace of the greens. At night the main topic of conversation among the caddies was who was going to play with whom, because once you got past Faldo and Woosnam and Seve and Olazabal things were very much up in the air. Howard Clark and Mark James as a team was a fairly popular guess so we weren't too far out when they announced the pairings.

On the morning of 21 September I went up to Seve's room to collect the clubs and save him carrying them down. We had been drawn against Tom Watson and Chip Beck, and Seve was in the best sort of mood – quietly confident and very relaxed – less nervous, in fact, than his caddie as it turned out!

When play began I found for the first time in a long while that my nerves were stretched a bit. We got off to a pretty good start in the match but on the second hole I picked the wrong sprinkler and Dave, Olazabal's caddie, said, 'I think you've got it wrong there, Ian. Do you want to recheck?' This wasn't too good a move to make in my first Ryder Cup and Seve noticed straight away.

'You're a bit nervous,' he said, which was good of him because he could have bawled me out for a basic error like that.

'I'm not too bad now,' I told him and he replied, 'OK, let's go then.'

Coming to the sixteenth we were all square and it was a very tight match, thanks mainly to Watson who had kept them in it. Beck, a fitness fanatic who looks like welded steel, was very nervous and didn't perform well at all. Seve missed a 6-footer and we went one down, but then he and Ollie showed real determination to get back level at the next. Ollie cut his drive into the bunker and Seve played out short, but then Jose-Maria holed the 20-footer to win the hole and take it to the last. On the last the wind was against and both pushed the ball out right. Left with too long a shot to carry the water, we laid up, and then both two putted for five and a half. The boys weren't too happy because they thought they should have won that, particularly as the only other points in the morning foursomes came from Faldo and Woosnam who halved with Kite and Curtis Strange to leave Europe 3–1 down.

But what a change there was in the afternoon. We

had Watson again, and Mark O'Meara and Ollie started off by sinking a good putt on the first. Confidence shot sky high and we knew we were going to do well. After five holes we were five up and the only real danger was getting too casual – you have to keep the thumbscrews on. Sure enough we lost the sixth and the Americans started a mini-comeback, yet slowly but surely, as the halved holes mounted, the pressure on them built up. As far as we caddies were concerned, we just wanted to get the match over, because two matches in a day were hard work and we were looking forward to putting the bags away and getting out to watch the other games.

At nine we were still four up and elsewhere Europe was up in three matches and level in another. The Spanish boys were really firing off each other now, and on thirteen Seve, who really had the bit between his teeth, actually drove the green. There were two officials standing on the front edge and as I handed him the driver I said, half jokingly, 'Just watch those two old blokes stood down there.' He hit his drive and it went straight between the two of them over 300 yards away. The match ended there and then when Seve sank a 3-footer back up the hill and they shook hands.

It was vital to get that first win to lift the rest of the team. The only problem was that we were at the furthest point of the course and we had to walk all the way back with the bags. Dave Renwick and I got back, ditched the bags and had a sandwich and a quick drink – which I think we deserved after thirty-one holes – and then dashed out again to cheer the others on. Apart from the European team and the Belfry crowd, a lot of other professionals turned up to root us on. Michael King, the former Ryder Cup player, followed a lot of the matches and I can recall seeing Mark Mouland and Chris Moody there, all great for morale.

And, of course, the team responded magnificently. Faldo and Woosie beat Mark Calcavecchia and McCumber two holes, but probably the best win came from the Scots, Sam Torrance and Gordon Brand Junior, who beat the very strong pairing of Curtis Strange and Paul Azinger on the last, much to the delight of the rest of the team spread round the eighteenth. Clark and James accounted for Freddy Couples and Wadkins easily and that was it, an afternoon whitewash.

It was a dream of a day. The gallery was fantastic and you couldn't have wished for better support. You knew everyone was going well by the roars coming from around the course. We had had the best possible start, leading 5–3, and we were all waiting to see the pairings for the next day.

Half an hour after the finish the captains announced the foursomes line-ups and we had got Kite and Curtis Strange! No motivation needed for Seve there. Jacklin kept him and Olazabal together because they seemed to bring out something extra special in each other and Faldo and Woosnam also went out unchanged. Jacklin's policy was to keep his strongest teams together, whereas Raymond Floyd, the American captain, liked to go round saying, 'I want everyone to get a game,' which sounds all right on the face of it but didn't work out in practice for him. He complained about Europe keeping their top partnerships together but there's nothing in the rules that says you can't do so.

Jacklin sent out Christy and Ronan Rafferty instead of Clark and James, but whereas Christy was playing well Rafferty was having an absolute nightmare with his putter and they were in dire straits. They scrambled a couple of holes towards the end of their match but really were never in it against Calc and Ken Green.

With Woosie and Faldo winning and the Scots going down, everything was keyed on the last match out, which was Seve and Ollie. It was vital to keep that two-point cushion and our game turned into a titanic struggle. Strange is as gritty as they come and Kite, too, was playing well; on form it was possibly the Americans' top pairing. By the tenth we had a two-hole lead but they came back with wins at fourteen and fifteen. After a half on sixteen Seve hit a good drive on seventeen, but then Ollie carved the second away to the right, leaving us tight up against a pine tree. In situations like that I would always fancy Seve to improvise something and get up close, but he had to pick the club up steeply and he caught it a bit too much into the ground and the ball popped straight into a bunker. Fortunately, Strange and Kite were having their own adventures with Curtis playing into a bunker and his partner playing out short, so when Ollie played out of the sand to 5 feet Seve had the putt for a five and a half and of course he stroked it in as cool as you like.

It was typical of the way the Spanish boys were complementing each other. One would make a bad shot and the other would get them out of it. So everything came down to the eighteenth and all the other Europeans were there rooting for us while the Americans were encouraging their pairing, for everyone had realized how vital this game was. The crowd were going absolutely berserk.

All week the eighteenth was to play a crucial role in the Ryder Cup and this day was no exception. It was playing par on this occasion but both teams found themselves in the same trap after their second shots. The pressure was obviously getting to Strange, because when he went in to play out he had a moan about the cameras going off whereas Ollie went in and splashed out to 8 feet. Kite missed his putt and Seve, to his obvious delight, sank his for the match. So there was the two-point cushion, an absolutely vital point for us – and just how vital was obviously appreciated by Strange, because he strode off without even shaking hands.

With the singles to be played on the last day, it was important to give everybody a game, so Canizares came in with Bernhard Langer. We had Calcavecchia and Green, and Mark James and Howard Clark had Payne Stewart and a smarting Curtis Strange – and what a tussle it was! We had a solid start again and by the turn the pressure was all on the Americans.

Seve and Ollie had played the tenth brilliantly all week. They had peppered the flag and never had anything worse than a birdie, but Seve pushed his drive out right and it clattered down right of the bunker, leaving him a difficult chip over the sand. I couldn't see any way he could get close, because it was a tight lie on very firm ground and there was very little room to the flag. But he played an absolutely amazing shot for a certain three and then cursed because it hadn't gone in the hole!

Ollie made his three, too, and then incredibly Calc three-putted and I knew he had gone. So instead of winning one in every three holes, they needed a win one in every two. But elsewhere we looked like taking a drubbing because Langer and Canizares were struggling – nothing would drop for them – and Woosie and Faldo were in trouble as well.

On fourteen Ollie sank a good putt for a two to

make it four up for us, but then came the news that Faldo and Woosie had lost to Chip Beck and Azinger and the Langer–Canizares match finished on seventeen and all the attention swung back to us and the James–Clark epic.

On fifteen Seve's putt rimmed the hole and came out again, and Mark Calcavecchia somewhat resignedly said, 'What are you doing – are you just toying with us or what?'

He needn't have worried, because the match finished at sixteen and we dashed over to see the thrilling climax to the final fourball.

On the fifteenth Mark and Howard had got it back to one down. James was in the bunker, but then just missed holing out and, of course, being Mark, was really upset because he missed it. However, Howard holed an 18-foot putt to make it all square.

After halves on the next two holes all four of them were in good shape after their drives on seventeen, yet incredibly both of the Americans carved their seconds away right into the plantation and when Howard holed his putt they had gone from two down to one up and the Americans were shattered. On the last Mark ran his third up to ½ inch and this time Curtis did shake hands. You could see the delight in the rest of the team – and everyone was there – because we had that two-point lead going into the singles and we needed just five points from the twelve matches to keep the cup. By now everyone was shattered mentally, but the James–Clark result had given the team a big boost.

Then Jacklin put his starting line-up on one sheet, Floyd put his on another and they put them both together. The number-one match was Paul Azinger against Seve Ballesteros.

That final morning was unbelievable. I picked up

the bag and went down to the practice area to find Seve there well ahead of me. The cheer the players received when they walked on to the practice ground was tremendous. Then blow me if the caddies didn't get a cheer as well! Seve was very relaxed: it was a beautiful day and we got just the start we wanted, going ahead after five, and Seve knew how vital it was to get that first point up on the board. But then Azinger holed one right off the green, won the next and by the eighth was one up. All of a sudden we were really struggling and Azinger was firing on all cylinders. He won nine and I had a horrible feeling then that not only were we going to lose our match but the cup as well, because after two hours of the singles Europe led in just one match and it was going to be an uphill battle.

But then on the tenth we got a bit of a break. Seve took a three wood and it went into the trees, landed on the bank and bounced on to the green. He putted up close and Azinger conceded. We took the eleventh too, to go back all square. On twelve, however, the game swung back the American's way. It's a long par three, but Seve hit it right down by the grandstand. He got a drop and chipped out well to about 3 feet, yet missed the putt. After two in a row the last thing you want to do is give one straight back, and while Azinger had gone one up his caddie suddenly decided he could do with some extra help on the next tee. Seve was getting ready to drive when the American caddie moved into his line of vision.

I said, 'Would you mind moving back?' and after pretending he couldn't hear he very begrudgingly moved back a couple of feet.

I asked him again a bit louder and a bit more aggressively and I have to admit there were a few things said that should not really have been required before he got out of the way.

A half on thirteen and then we pulled one back on fourteen. It was 174 metres to the flag that day and Seve played a pretty good four iron to about 6 metres behind the flag.

I thought, 'Right, here's half a chance,' and sure enough Azinger botched his putt and Seve saw his opportunity and knocked it straight in: all square, and that must have been a great lift to everyone on the course.

Sadly, there was no helping poor Howard Clark who conceded on the eleventh, and suddenly the first point was up there to America. Kite had won eight and seven, and to see a drubbing like that must have done them a lot of good. Fortunately for us, a couple of our more senior citizens were still hanging in there.

Seve seemed to be running out of luck, however. On fifteen he played two good shots to leave a gentle run up to the green, but he couldn't get it on the top level and his putt stopped 6 inches short. I thought a half was a certainty because Azinger was over the green on the fringe. But he took an iron and bladed it out at 100 miles an hour. The ball hit the hole and went in for a win. If it had missed it would have finished off the top level. One down and three to play!

We had halves on sixteen and seventeen and once again it was down to what was now becoming the famous – or infamous – eighteenth. Azinger hit his drive into the water and we got on to the bank on the far side and I thought, 'Cracked it!'

Crossing over the bridge, I bumped into Bruce Rioch, the Middlesbrough manager, which was a nice surprise although we didn't have much time to talk about Boro's results.

When we got to the ball I worked out the yardage and saw that it was 165 to the front and 196 to the flag.

Seve said, 'Three iron.'

'Don't you think you could get there with a four? You're coming out of a bit of grass and could do with the loft.'

'No, I'm happy with a three.'

While we were having a discussion over the club, Azinger was taking a drop in what looked like a pretty favourable position as most players had had to drop way back, so Seve went over and gave everyone his opinion on where the ball crossed before Azinger hit a great wood into the bunker on the left-hand side of the green.

Seve had a basic shot over the water but, as everyone knows by now, he hit it half-way up the ball and bounced it straight into the lake. He was absolutely seething, and as we walked over to where the ball had gone in he said, 'Make sure you get the yardage right on this one, because it will be the first you've got right all day.'

I checked everything off and he double-checked, and I gave him the nine iron. He pitched it on the upslope and it started to spin back and I was thinking, 'That has to be perfect,' when it stopped, leaving a long putt down the slope.

By now Seve was boiling, and I recognized the symptoms and got out of the way. Azinger played well out of the bunker and really I didn't care to watch any more because the only chance Seve had was to hole the putt. It was about as difficult as you could get, down the bank out of the shadow and into the sunlight, and he gave it the full treatment, prowling round, checking and rechecking, and then he hit it with quite a bit of pace. It picked up speed down the bank and in it went – if he'd missed, it would have gone 6 feet past. All hell broke loose.

I'd gone by this stage and I didn't dare watch Azinger's putt because we'd wanted to go through undefeated and I didn't think we deserved less than a half, but Azinger knocked it in perfectly.

Seve was shattered and I let him go off. I went to the player's lounge to see Lesley. I felt terrible: it wasn't just losing the match – it was letting the team down. At that stage we had lost three in a row with Langer going down three and two to Beck and we were in serious trouble. Back in the clubhouse my frustration boiled over and I picked up Seve's bag and threw it against the wall. Then I remembered: 'His watch!' and dashed over to see if I'd broken it – that really would have made his day. I sat down and all the tension and adrenalin overflowed into tears. I had a couple of halves and Lesley was trying to console me when in walked Seve.

'Come on, we have to get out there and start rooting for the rest of them,' he said. Somehow he had managed to lift himself and he did the same for me. I took the bags up to the room and then went out to sit by the eighteenth. What I saw there I will never forget.

We were still three down and it was tight in all the others, but Jose-Maria Olazabal birdied seventeen to go all square with Payne Stewart, so that was all down to the last too. Ollie drove safely over the water, but Stewart splashed down in the drink then, incredibly, tried to play it out of the water, not once but three times, and that was one match pulled back because Ollie just knocked it on to the green safely to finish the cup undefeated.

Seve now seemed to cheer up and he said, 'It's going to be tight, but we can still do it.'

Rafferty and Calcavecchia were next up eighteen all square and again, amazingly, the American drove into the water, took a drop and put the next one in too. Ronan just stood there in the middle of the fairway until Calc walked over, shook his hand and called it a day. Rafferty had played excellently and it was nice to see him do well as he had been desperately disappointed with his form up to then. It was great, too, because his mother had come over from Ulster to see him.

Suddenly the crowd woke up again and I dashed off to see the Couples–O'Connor match as that was going to be the next decisive one. Then Mark James beat Mark O'Meara at the sixteenth and we had three points up on the board and we had answered them right back.

On sixteen Couples missed a birdie chance and Christy had a putt from 3 feet for the half. Well, he gave it an almighty whack and it nearly missed on the right, committed suicide at the last minute and dived in the hole. The crowd went wild: Christy is the type of character they take to their heart – everybody loves him.

Looking up at the scoreboard, we saw Canizares come back to all square against Ken Green, and Seve, who really had a smile back on his face by now, dashed off to encourage his countryman.

On seventeen Fred Couples was red-hot favourite because he boomed a superb drive out, and after both had gone through the green with their seconds Christy mishit his little run down and finished 10 or 11 feet short. He missed that and Fred had a 4-footer to win there and then. Everyone was expecting it to go in, but he pushed it out and the nerves were stretched like elastic bands – it was almost unbearable.

Gordon Brand Junior was on a bit of a charge by then, and Nick Faldo, who had been three shots down, started to pull back on Lanny Wadkins and the pendulum began to swing back the way of Europe.

But then Couples hit the longest drive of the week over the water at eighteen to find a perfect position with just an eight iron in. Christy had a long iron from a long way back and I was watching from the eighteenth green as he played up. To me it was one of the greatest shots ever under pressure, because he pitched it into the bank on the front and it ran up to within 5 feet. Fred must have cracked completely because he shot his eight iron straight out right and couldn't even find the green.

Canizares had got back all square a hole behind and suddenly it was all down to the oldest men on either team. Couples chipped down and couldn't get within 6 feet, missed the putt and shook hands. Christy just broke down on the green. It was a tremendously emotional moment because, at forty-one, he would probably never get another Ryder Cup and we all dashed out to congratulate him.

I said, 'Brilliant, Christy, absolutely brilliant,' but he was completely shattered. Then Freddie Couples' wife came over to give Christy a cuddle, and I thought that was a tremendous gesture. Everybody was swept away on a tide of emotion. I'd been sitting with Michael King, who is quite a tough nut, and he turned to me and said, 'I do believe I'm getting a bit emotional here, Ian.' Sure enough, I could see the tears in his eyes.

Then it was all down to forty-two-year-old Canizares, who had just scraped into the team with a fifth place in the German Open and who has dodgy eyesight anyway – really you couldn't have written the finale better as a work of fiction, because there caddying with him was Tom, my room-mate, who now had the chance of getting the point that would keep us the cup! Green had a longish second shot in and he hit the bank on the middle level and rolled back down to the bottom tier. Canny played an iron in but overshot and finished up at the back not far from where Seve had been but a much longer putt. He judged it perfectly, however, and ran it down to within 3 feet, a tremendous shot under that sort of pressure. Green charged his up the slope, missed coming back and Canny then had his 3-footer to keep the Ryder Cup.

In it went and Canizares, who is one of the most subdued men on a golf course, took off on a victory jig. Ollie got to him first, followed by Ronan and Seve. Tom, the caddie who never smiles, had a huge grin on his face, and all the clouds had lifted. The two veterans, and the most unlikely people to expect a result from, had retained the Ryder Cup for Europe.

Almost inevitably the rest was an anti-climax. We needed half a point to win outright, but it just wouldn't come. Gordon Brand Junior hit his ball on to the grandstand roof on the last and it rebounded into a bunker. He couldn't get up and down from there. Then, just after Concorde had flown over dipping its wings ready to take the Americans home, Sam Torrance, who had been overcome with emotion at the news of Canizares' win, lost to Tom Watson. Faldo bumped into the water on the last to hand it to Wadkins, and then finally Curtis Strange, who was playing for pride, having had a pretty bad week, beat Ian Woosnam by two holes and the match finished tied at 14–14.

We had been on three different levels of emotion that day. At one point we had felt terrible because we were getting pasted, then there had been the recovery and the elation of retaining the Ryder Cup, and finally it had all gone a bit flat. But then someone pointed out that this had been one of the strongest teams ever from America and the bookies had all made them favourites; we had gone in as underdogs. It was, therefore, still a great result. So with that excuse we went off to the players' lounge where the beer and the champagne flowed. By eight o'clock, when we set off for home, my voice had gone with singing so much.

There has been nothing before or since to take you up and down like the Ryder Cup. I can still remember walking down the eighteenth in the Open at Lytham. There was great emotion there too, but nothing to match that inspired by the different daily swings in fortune of team golf. Much was made of the crowd's bias the last time the event was in Europe, but in 1989 the fans at The Belfry were wonderful and totally non-partisan. They were as fair as they could be and it was thanks to them that our team raised their game to the extent they did.

After the champagne it was back to flat beer in many ways. Two weeks later we missed the cut in the German Masters at Monsheim and Seve decided to wind the season up at the Suntory at Wentworth. The sight of Chip Beck in the quarter-final inspired him to a 9 and 8 win, but then Nick Faldo beat us almost as one-sidedly 6 and 5 in the semi-final. Overall that year we had one marvellous week of golf of the standard you expect from Seve, two fighting wins; the rest were very poor results. I'm still convinced today that after the virus he picked up in America he was never the same. He showed good warm-up and preparation form, but he seemed to get tired in a lot of tournaments, especially in the third or fourth rounds.

At Augusta he had had a near-miss, yet that, I think, was sheer will power on his part to get in a winning position, the determination of a proud man, Seve would always give it his best shot, like the best in the world he is, even if he didn't feel 100 per cent. I firmly believe that if there is one man who can do the modern-day Grand Slam of all four Majors it's Seve Ballesteros. If he gets into a run of form as he has done in the past, he is quite capable of winning three, four or five tournaments spaced out over a year – as the Majors are.

After Wentworth, Seve took off to his home in Santander, but work for his caddie went on. At the end of the year I flew out to La Manga in Cartagena, Spain, for the players' school and a look at the less glamorous side of the pro golf circuit. The school is for players who haven't finished in the top 120 on the money list, for up-and-coming stars who need to get a card and even for players who have had a card for a number of years or have had to withdraw because of illness or injury.

It starts with pre-qualifying and finishes with 200 people playing off for the fifty cards available, so it's very cut-throat: six consecutive rounds of golf with possible heartbreak at the end of them. I carried for Andy Cotton and happily he managed to get his card and there was great satisfaction in helping him round. Andy's dream came true and in 1990 he was qualified to join the PGA tour, one of the greatest sporting shows on earth.

10

Broken Dreams

IAN WOOSNAM HAS TWICE topped golf's money list in Europe since turning professional in 1976. At the age of thirty-three he will probably never want for anything again. However, like every other professional golfer, like Seve and Olazabal, Faldo and Lyle, he had to earn a player's card, and it took little Woosie three attempts to get through this annual ritual of happiness, frustration and heartbreak. Because, make no mistake, the ten days at players' school, where 200 hopefuls fight for just fifty cards, are the toughest any potential tournament player will face anywhere. You get the players who put up a real battle and manage to obtain a card, and the relief on their faces is heartwarming. But you also see the other side where a player will slump off after throwing everything away on the final few holes.

I recall one player walking off at La Manga after missing his card, having a few drinks in the restaurant at the clubhouse there, then taking all his clubs out one by one and breaking the shafts over his knee. This memory sums up the frustration of the game, the torment all players have to go through to get on the tour and set off on the road to fame, perhaps having only one chance to try for it.

The quest for a card is like a mass game of 'Devil take the hindmost'. There are six rounds of golf and the first cut-off comes after four rounds with the top 100 players and ties going through to fight for the fifty cards. Surprisingly, despite the cut-throat nature of players' school, it's all quite friendly, but in my opinion it's the hardest week in a player's life, two tournaments rolled into one mass of stress and strain with potential oblivion waiting at the end. The mixture of competitors is always the same: the established club professionals, the new men coming in, guys who have turned professional but failed to retain a card on the European tour, players who haven't made enough money to keep their cards. Look down the list and you will see a lot of names who once promised so much and delivered comparatively little. There are some famous names there, tournament winners who know exactly what to expect, but there are also some absolute greenhorns who come out badly advised and with little idea of what is involved. They come with their Mums and Dads and families, in pairs, in fours or in groups, and in all shapes and sizes.

I go to the school because it is a good week for me with the yardage books, but also because I enjoy trying to help some of the lesser lights make the grade. Sometimes I don't know whether to laugh or cry at some of the sights I see there.

In 1990 they moved the school from its established base in La Manga and took it down to Montpelier in France to Massane and La Grande-Motte. They were different tests of golf altogether. The year before at

La Manga minus two earned a card, but at Massane it was plus nine. It was a much sterner proposition, but much fairer too, in my opinion, because a lot of players were getting too used to La Manga.

The following illustrates perfectly the tragi-comic nature of players' school, and to save embarrassment I won't mention the name of the player involved. Dad was caddying for his son and they were standing on the seventeenth tee at Massane. It's quite a long hole for a par three and plays about 200 yards, but it was downwind on this occasion.

Now quite often a player won't talk to his caddie – he'll signal to him and the caddie will signal back. Son looked across to Dad and signalled questioningly with four fingers. Dad looked back, shook his head and signalled five. The player shook his head, showed four fingers again and mouthed the word 'Four'. He then took out his four iron, presuming Dad had wanted him to take the five, and because of that he hit the shot a bit easy and finished about 20 yards short of the green.

He walked straight over to his Dad, slammed the club back into the bag and said, 'Bloody hell, Dad, I could have taken a three iron there!'

'Why didn't you then?' asked Dad.

'But you signalled a five,' said the exasperated lad.

'No, Son, I was signalling that after bogeying the hole before you were *five* over.'

There's a little lesson here: if the player had had a professional caddie, the misunderstanding probably wouldn't have happened. They would have been on the same wavelength, whereas in this case player and caddie weren't exactly thinking on the same lines. Dad was concentrating on how many shots his son was over par when he should have had his mind on the job and thinking club.

That same year one poor old guy was setting up over the ball near a lake and, as he began his backswing, toppled slowly over into it. He had to be hauled out by a PGA official. My player that year, Mark Foreman, seemed to suffer a rush of blood whenever he saw water. Every time we got to the par five fifth, in he'd go and we had a couple of sevens there. On the seventh, too, another hole surrounded by water, he took seven. Basically the problem wasn't the water, however – it was not playing enough golf that year. He didn't have a safety shot in his bag and just wasn't confident standing over the ball. It cost him six shots, and that's a lot in three holes. He missed qualifying by three shots.

Some of the blokes out at players' school live on a shoestring because it's an expensive business, costing around £2,000 minimum if you include accommodation and travel, and for a lot of them this sort of cash is very difficult to find. They not only need money before the start, they need it just to play the qualifying rounds too. Then, of course, they need even more to start playing the tour. It takes a very special, very tough character to succeed, but knowing you have come through all that and survived must be a very good feeling.

Sometimes the pressures are also on the parents accompanying their hopeful offspring. There was one young lad, Jimmy White from Scotland, who had his Dad caddying for him in 1990. Jimmy looked like blowing it in the last round. He was going along quite merrily, making the cut at about plus four, when all of a sudden he dropped four in a row to go eight over. But he proved a battler and started back birdie, birdie, birdie, par to make the cut, and Dad was leaping about all over the place.

I said to him, 'Dad, caddies are supposed to show a bit of calm and decorum on the golf course.'

Back came the reply, 'I'll show you some calm and decorum . . . in the bar afterwards!'

Success was important to both of them, because if Jimmy had failed he would have finished up on the dole; now, however, he could play the Tartan Tour in 1991. Some players take failure well, others just collapse – they don't have a clue what they are going to do or how they are going to make ends meet until the same time the following year when they will go through it all again.

You see a lot of tears at players' school: tears of joy as well as the other kind. But probably one of the biggest smiles I can recall belonged to young John Phillip Price, the Welsh lad who holed a birdie putt on the last to finish plus one and earn the second card. On the other side of the coin, there was the Aussie David Ecob who missed a 12-inch putt to miss his card by one shot. Such are the margins between joy and heartbreak in professional golf.

A lot of the players at school I have come across regularly over the years, which makes their triumphs or disasters even more poignant for me. I've known Haydn Green for ten years, going back to the days when, as a skinny little kid with black-rimmed glasses, he used to play for the Cleveland Salver back home. Now he's six feet of beefcake and wears contact lenses, and when he arrived at Montpelier in 1990 he had the new Mrs Green in tow. Haydn was actually on his honeymoon and played the qualifying, the pre-qualifying, everything, with his bride carrying his bag. She had even given up her job to try to help him get his card. They struggled round to the last eighteen holes and he had to play the last four under the most severe pressure imaginable. He went double bogey, birdie, bogey, birdie, then got up and down out of the bunker on the last to make his card. Mrs Green's face was a picture.

The twentieth card that year went to Donald Stirling, the first man I ever caddied for officially on tour. He had suffered seven years of trials and tribulations since, having had to give up the pro's job at Harrogate and had domestic problems, but then decided golf was the thing he was best at and bounced back to get a place on tour.

There were the lads from the Walker Cup team like Andy Harefield who, even with Andy Prodger working for him, could only finish fifty-ninth, and a further sad exclusion for me was Philip Harrison, for whom I had also caddied in the early days.

We had another first that year when the first ever Norwegian, Per Haugsrud, won a card, but there were also the sad sights of some past tournament winners struggling and failing. Robert Lee, once one of the brightest of British prospects, managed to survive. However, the 1989 school winner, Hans Peter Thuel of Germany, who had only made £6,000 on the tour and had had to go back to school, missed out completely at number fifty-five. He was actually one shot off being tied for forty-sixth place but his 442 took him outside the fifty. It was that close. Jeff Hall, a former Jersey Open winner, was 201st and didn't even make the final two days; and Noel Ratcliffe, once good enough to win the Benson and Hedges at Fulford, was seventy-sixth.

Whether they will be back again I don't know. All I do know is that anyone who goes through players' school, even once, deserves all the credit in the world.

11

Playing Partners

THE END OF THE RAINBOW for every man at players' school, of course, is the chance to join the tour and rub shoulders with the elite – perhaps to win a tournament, even make a million. I can appreciate these aspirations, since carrying the bag for the best golfer in the world has taken me to every major course and to every tournament that matters. It has also given me the opportunity to see close at hand Seve's friends, rivals and the occasional enemy among the world's top golfers.

On the whole, golf being the correct, disciplined and gentlemanly game it is, it produces characters to match. However, I wouldn't say I have liked everyone with whom I have worked. There are people I wouldn't, for example, go for a night out with and I've tended to get along with them because I was there doing a job. When the job is done, you tend to disappear in different directions. There are others I wouldn't work for, full stop, but some I'd go out with tomorrow.

On the circuit at the moment one man who does

stand out as a genuine nice guy, as his caddie Dave Musgrove will testify, is Sandy Lyle. He is quite a chum of Seve's, too, so I've seen a lot of him, and what you notice above all is how easy-going he is on a golf course. There's always the feeling that he is just going along with 75 per cent effort, but of course there is immense power there, particularly with that famous one iron which he will use just like a driver and get the same distance as a lot of other people using a wood. Sandy is the true gentle giant, ultra-relaxed but, as he has shown in the past and will I'm sure again in the future, there is a killer instinct lurking under that gentle exterior. He is just as determined as the next man to do well, yet he doesn't appear to become pent up or get the adrenalin flowing as someone like Seve does. Sandy calls himself a Scot, but I always tend to think of him as the perfect, calm, cool, English gentleman out for a game in the park on a Sunday afternoon.

The opposite to Sandy in many ways is Nick Faldo who *always* looks as though he's there to win. Nick is probably technically the most correct player on the circuit, having worked for so long and so hard on a swing that always stands up under pressure. He is very much a lone wolf and, I must admit, a very hard man to talk to. Whenever I have spoken to him we have always got on, but I know that over the years his caddie, Andy Prodger, has had some very hard times with Nick. When they came back from Australia in January 1990, after perhaps the most successful year you could wish for, Nick gave Andy the sack, which seemed pretty diabolical to me at the time. Faldo said the two 'weren't communicating', yet Andy is one of the best caddies in the world, very knowledgeable on the game and technique and also one of the most inoffensive characters around. At the time it came as a big shock, but then again perhaps it wasn't too surprising because Nick has had a couple of caddie changes and it doesn't seem to matter whether he's successful with them or not – in the end there's just something that makes him show them the door for no apparent reason. It will be interesting to see how long Fanny Sunesson lasts on the Faldo bag.

Nick has had a long-standing rivalry with Sandy and he has had the occasional brush with Seve over the years too. Basically he and Seve get on together, but there has been the odd problem.

I like to call Ian Woosnam 'Mr Pocket Battleship', because he is the ultimate fighter. He has worked very hard to get to the top and deserves all the success in the world. Ian is never a man to take lightly, because he can be playing a little bit off and then he'll spark, and he never quits until the nineteenth hole. He is a great character and a great patriot, the type you always want on your side in a scrap, as he has shown in the Ryder Cup time and again. Occasionally he makes the game look ridiculously easy with that free swing of his. He had a frustrating phase for a year or so – he changed clubs and put on a bit of weight, but then he got back in shape and that first Major can't be far away now.

Christy O'Connor, known as 'Junior' to distinguish him from his well-known uncle, became a national hero overnight with that famous second shot to the eighteenth in the Ryder Cup against Fred Couples. Christy is one of the characters of the tour, a man who can always be relied upon to brighten a dull moment. I don't think I'm speaking out of turn when I say he has been known to like a drink, and when he has had one he can be really entertaining.

On the course he has great determination and a lot

of guile. He well deserved his place at The Belfry and then produced the goods with the most incredible shot under pressure, and most people will tell you it couldn't have happened to a nicer guy. Even Christy will admit that it came at the tail end of his career, but it could just rejuvenate him . . . although I don't think you'll find him jogging up and down in the rain on a fitness campaign. Like his famous uncle, and most of the Irish lads for that matter, Christy is a great wind player. We went round with Christy Senior once over in Ireland and when the wind got up he still had all the shots – he could make that ball sing in the wind.

Des Smyth is another who comes into that category; a bit of breeze and he's an absolute magician. Des has had some bad luck with illness and injuries, but he is another determined character, another scrapper, at the same time being a great guy to get along with. He has an individual swing which works well for him and he makes a steady living out of the game and can always be relied upon to pop up and win the odd tournament. Des is also unusual because he has been with the same caddie, John, for eight or nine years, although he still has a long way to go to catch Jimmy Cousins who has had fifteen seasons with Manuel Pinero.

Ronan Rafferty has come on strongly over the last few seasons and in 1989 had a fantastic year. He played some very consistent golf all the way through and finished top of the order of merit. Ronan seems to have learned to schedule his season a bit better lately – at one time he was a golfaholic. You'd find him in every tournament every week of the year, but now he has begun to pace himself better. I think he has stepped back and looked at his future overall and realized that the occasional rest can only help. Ronan, like a lot of youngsters in the game, has been known to show the odd flash of temperament, but there's more maturity there now and I can see him being a winner for a lot of years to come.

You can't miss Sam Torrance on the circuit, particularly when he gets on the green with that giant putter. Sam has had his problems with his game, but he is still one of the best strikers of the ball around. It's when he gets on the putting surface that his troubles start. Now he has adopted that ultra-long putter, but personally I think all his problems are in the head. His wife Suzanne was a very pleasant addition to the circuit and I will always remember the two of them sitting by the putting green at St Nom la Breteche drinking champagne in the sun. It seemed like a good idea at the time! Suzanne is a smashing lass and, like most of the other wives, she follows Sam round the circuit come rain or shine.

There are two Gordon Brands on the tour. They are not related and really you couldn't find two more different characters, but then Gordon J. Brand, the Yorkshire version, is in a class of his own. Seve has a golf exhibition in which he likes to impersonate a lot of golfers – like little Woosie, for instance, when he will drop on his knees and play shots. He also does Arnold Palmer and he does a great take-off of Gordon J. in which he stops completely at the top of his backswing.

Gordon J. has the driest sense of humour. We'll be wandering round the golf course with him when all of a sudden he'll come out with the 'Brand' joke, one of the most unbelievably silly you've ever heard. He used to have a book full of them. My best friend, Roy Holland, caddies for him – and talk about two opposites: the unflappable and the completely flappable!

Gordon J. broke his duck in 1989 with his first tour

win in thirteen seasons at the Belgian Open and it was really deserved. He finished second to Greg Norman in the 1986 Open and never got the recognition he ought to have had for that. Along with Mark James and Ken Brown, he is one of the best links players in Britain.

The other Gordon Brand, now known as 'Junior', is said by some to look like me, although I always tell him I'm the better-looking one of the two! Brand Junior is a great player and should be around in the Ryder Cup team for a long time to come. He has suffered a bit from lack of confidence, I feel, because so often he has got into a winning position then hasn't been able to go through with it. Like Gordon J. he is something of a character and always good for a laugh. He represents Scotland, although he has a pretty pukka English accent, rather like Sandy.

I had the pleasure of caddying for Mark James when he shot 82 in the first English Open, but then Mark is the sort of player who will shoot 82 one day and 62 the next. Well known for walking round a course looking as if someone's just burgled his house, underneath that miserable-looking exterior he's probably laughing and joking his head off, because he is another of the great characters of the tour. Mark has a very individual style and has worked hard for his successes. When he's firing on all cylinders he can play some superb golf.

Another player who is often misunderstood, or has been in the past, is Ken Brown. He has a reputation for being 'Mr Slowcoach' and the Press blew one or two incidents involving him out of all proportion, because again he is a smashing guy. I enjoy talking to him and having a laugh. He always calls me 'Irony' as once when we were over in France some French fan was trying to call out my name and all he could manage was

'Irony' so that stuck. Ken has been around for a long time and after failing to fulfil his potential in the USA looks as though he is going to concentrate on Europe in the future – and he has the ability to do it. There's more fat on a greasy chip in Ken's case, but I don't think that has ever held him back, particularly when he's on the green.

'Sir' Neil Coles MBE we don't see all that much of, mainly because he doesn't like flying so doesn't get to many tournaments, but it hasn't stopped him doing a lot for European golf in his capacity as chairman of the PGA tour. Neil has a very dry sense of humour and he and his wife make a lovely couple. As a golfer he is another who can invent shots, a man who can work the ball as they say. One of my favourite recollections of Neil is when he was at tournament in Germany some years ago and holed in one at the sixteenth to win a car. All I could hear was Mrs Coles – probably the only spectator following that match – screaming and shouting at the top of her voice, 'It's gone in the hole! It's gone in the hole!' Neil was another who never got the plaudits he deserved for his third place in the Open in 1961 and his runner-up spot to Tom Weiskopf in 1973. As in the case of Gordon J. Brand, no one seems to remember who was second.

Of the overseas players, Greg Norman is rated a top bag by the caddies because he is reputed to pay the highest percentages but, as with Seve, you have to work extremely hard for them. Again like Seve, he can be all right for most of the time and then explode. Greg has tremendous power, but having watched him throw away a couple of tournaments I've often wondered a bit about his make-up. In 1989 there were a couple of bad decisions on clubs at crucial times. At the Masters, coming to the eighteenth, I think I would have asked him to take a driver off the tee because he could have knocked it left of the trap and still have had a short iron into the flag, instead of which he took two irons and it cost him a bogey and a place in the play-off. Then at the Troon Open the same year he thundered a drive 310 yards down the last into a bunker when, with his power, a one iron would have been sufficient to get the ball down the right half even into the light rough and still have a shot at the flag. It's all in the mind, and you have to ask, 'Does he stay calm and calculating at the right time?' – because ultimately there's only one man who makes the final decision and it's not the caddie.

The man in my book who will be the next superstar is Jose-Maria Olazabal. When he's on his game he looks to have everything with no real flaws. He fires those irons in close when he sees the chance and that is the real secret. He and Seve make a formidable pair, as the Americans found in the Ryder Cup. They seem to set a spark going in each other and the result can be some truly outstanding golf. Ollie's caddie, Dave Renwick, is Scottish, and while they rabbit away to each other in Spanish they have to change to English to talk to us, which can create some amusing situations. Ollie is a very quiet guy and you rarely see him off the course, although you can't miss his manager, Sergio, who has trimmed down nicely to about 20 stones these days.

Jose-Maria Canizares was renowned a few years ago for some tremendous bursts with the putter which would give him incredibly low scores. That was before the Ryder Cup in 1989 when, as the oldest man on either team, he came up with the win that retained the cup and made himself the most unexpected hero. That putt will stay in my mind for a long time because it was really quick downhill and he had to come off the top level. As we all know by now, he got it pin high. The dance of joy he did when he holed out will always be one of my warmest memories in golf.

I've often had a quiet chuckle to myself when I've seen Pete Coleman, Bernhard Langer's caddie, struggling round with his bag. I'd hate to guess how many sets of clubs Bernhard has had in his career and Pete has often had to cart round twenty-six or twenty-seven clubs, four putters, two sets of irons and a couple of drivers. I'm surprised Pete hasn't slipped a disc and I've even known Willie Hoffman, Bernhard's manager, bring out another set of irons to try.

Bernhard is the workaholic of the tour. He has had problems with his health and his back but his will power and determination have kept him going. I will never forget one round with Bernhard at El Saler in Spain when I was caddying for Brian Marchbank. It's a long, testing course and there was a bit of a wind but Bernhard shot a 62 and probably one of the finest rounds I've ever seen. Every iron he played just covered the flag and dropped next to the pin: tremendous.

Bernhard may be outwardly serious but he is a great character underneath. At Biarritz once I was walking past this pot bunker and he was approaching in the other direction. When we got level he just gave me a push, watched me disappear down this pothole, then walked away laughing.

One of the biggest hitters on the tour is Jumbo Osaki. I don't know if he's called Jumbo because of his size or the size of his trousers – they are certainly the baggiest I've ever seen. If a strong wind got up he would make a perfect kite. But Jumbo is a very good player and could get close to a Major one of these days.

Of the Americans, one of my favourites is Fred Couples, otherwise known as 'Boom Boom'. I've been out with Fred a few times and he hits the ball amazing distances but seems to have trouble when he gets to the putting green. He doesn't seem to make the scores his golf merits. Fred is a really nice guy and he has always said I could work for him if I was over in the States.

I regret in many ways missing Palmer, Trevino and Nicklaus in their heyday. We have had a few practice rounds with Lee and I won't forget his opening round in the 1989 Masters when he was leading. Nicklaus I would like to have watched at first hand, but then since I've been with the man who is the next best I'm not really sorry.

Despite all the vagaries of 1989, a year in which Seve finished only eighth in the Order of Merit, I was convinced that 1990 would see the dawn of a new decade of Seve swashbuckling. At Wentworth he had simply said, 'See you next year,' and I gave him a ring in December to check not only the dates for 1990 but also that I was still on the bag. When he took me on he had said, 'You have the job until there is a major disaster.' I often wondered what he considered a major disaster. In the event, 1990 turned into a catalogue of disaster.

12

Suddenly, Last Summer

My LAST SUMMER with Seve Ballesteros began on 17 February 1990 with a flight from Teesside at 6.50 am for the Middle East and the Emirates Airline Desert Classic at the Emirates Golf Club in Dubai.

Before the tournament began there was some hard bargaining to be done. With £275,000 in prize money at stake and the tournament taking place in one of the most affluent countries in the world, I thought it would be as good a time as any to tackle Seve about a pay rise. I hadn't had one for two years and the price of everything, especially air travel, had gone up. I knew it was going to be a tough job because Seve, to put it mildly, is pretty tight with a buck.

Joe Collet had met me at the airport and told me, 'Seve wants you at the course at 11 am on Sunday.'

What course? All I could see was sand, although I presumed they would be all right for filling the bunkers. The taxi to the course went straight through the middle of what looked like a set for *Lawrence of Arabia*, when all of a sudden I spotted this white building in the distance and the driver said, 'Golf course!' It was just like a mirage, a fenced-off piece of green in the middle of the dunes and a beautiful, very well-tended, American-style golf lay-out.

Seve seemed in good form when I met him. He was playing the film star with the leading role in his own video which they were just finishing off as I arrived. At practice he was still in a good mood: time to ask about the money! I wanted a £50 a week rise, which he thought too much, but then he would, wouldn't he? Talk about drawing teeth! He was a bit reluctant, to put it mildly, and the bargaining became first warm, then heated. After half an hour he started to bend a little – even he was no match for a Yorkshireman. Finally he agreed.

'You're a very hard man,' he told me.

I retorted, 'If I'm hard I hate to think what you are.'

But I got the fifty quid and we shook on it. It was quite a help really, because I had to cover all my expenses myself, and while I'd often tried to talk him into some sort of assistance with flights he would never wear it. For a man of his means you wouldn't have thought it would have made any difference; if he paid all the expenses he could claim them against tax. But there again, I had always got a good percentage off him and it paid to remember that.

After practice I sweated my way round doing the yardage books and met Terry Duffy, the guy in charge of the tournament, a smashing bloke.

On the Wednesday in the Pro Am we were playing with three airline pilots and one of them seemed to be having trouble with his eyesight. 'Where's the flag?' he kept asking and I remember thinking, 'Remind me never to fly with him.' I think the pilot flew the Prince of Dubai around from oilfield to oilfield. Seve shot 71, quite a steady start, and his form was looking good.

On tournament day we drew Mark James and Gordon J. Brand, two great characters and relaxing playing partners, but Seve fired 72: not too promising.

On the Friday we got to five under after fourteen but then on fifteen we took a wrong club and made bogey. A par-bogey-par finish left us minus three and tied ninth and in fair shape. A win would have been nice to kick off the year, but a last-round 70 gave us third place with my former employer, Eamonn Darcy, picking up the winner's cheque.

Las Brisas and the American Express Mediterranean Open the week after brought back some happy memories as it was the place where I had had the first fateful conversation with Seve. I flew down to London and then joined the jet set when I boarded Seve's private jet to fly over to Marbella ... just me, Seve and his family and a couple of other Spanish golfers. They were staying at the golf club, so they dropped me off in the car at my hotel in Marbella: not a bad old life, but I had learned as a golf caddie that you can come down off that cloud very quickly.

Sure enough, in the Pro Am on the Wednesday we were three over on the front nine, five under for the back nine and had a minus two total, but then the weather turned nasty and we got the bad half of the draw to go with it. The cold afternoon and a 74 didn't make Seve any happier. We just made the cut and then the weather got worse along with the morale. It was wet and windy and Seve was putting to match it. A 73 left us tied fourteenth. It could have been worse, but not much.

From the mainland it was straight over to Palma, Majorca, for the Open Renault de Baleares at Son

Vida – or rather, not so straight. It was a 5 am start from Malaga to Barcelona, then from Barcelona to Palma, arriving at 11.35 am. This left me just enough time to sort out an apartment to stay in and measure the course. I managed to finish by 5 in the evening, Damon was there with me and, while he went for a swim, Dad put his feet up for a well-earned rest.

Next day I had to be up at 7.15 for Seve's usual 9.30 practice round. In the Pro Am he shot a 67, five under, and seemed more relaxed. Perhaps we were going to have a good week?

Seve turned up on the Thursday with a heavy cold but then proceeded to take the course by storm: six birdies, no bogeys. It was a perfect start, but my biggest concern was trying to avoid catching his cold. Fat chance! By the following day I was loaded to the eyeballs with medications, plus a couple of hankies and a supply of sweets. He was feeling better, I was feeling awful, but we sniffled and sucked our way round to a 66, two shots behind Magnus Persson – my old bosses were everywhere!

Out with Magnus next day we shot a 70, two under. Seve played poorly from 40 metres in, didn't chip too well, not like his famous short game at all, but Magnus started to look a bit shaky over the last few holes and I thought, 'Get a good start on the last day, put the pressure on him and we're in with a chance.'

We birdied the first, bogeyed the second after he got a flier and cleared the green. After nine we were sixteen under, still trailing, but two birdies on eleven and thirteen put us one behind Magnus coming to eighteen. That was when Magnus slipped up. The last is a long, slightly dogleg par five and with a good drive you can get far enough down to get on in two. Magnus played safe with an iron and left himself too much to do with his second. Seve found sand with his second but chipped out and holed for birdie. All square and it was back down the fairway to the eighteenth tee for the play-off. Magnus called right, showed he had learned his lesson by taking a metal wood ... and dumped it in the water on the left! Seve's one iron, four iron and two putts meant we had come from six behind to win the tournament, and I could start thinking with some optimism about the Masters and the first Major of the year.

By mid-March things may have been bucking up for the player, but the caddie was really in the wars. Playing golf at Cleveland I hurt my back, so it was more tablets (some for the back and some for the cold) and I hoped fervently that there were no drug tests for caddies in America! Nonetheless I reflected that I'd been lucky will illness, having suffered nothing serious over the years, which was important – because no carry, no money. This would be the first time I'd been ill during a tournament and it would be no joke carting round a 40 lb bag with a pain in the back. In America you need to be fit and on top of things as the humidity can really make it hard for you.

I managed to rise at 5.20 am to get organized and catch the 6.25 British Midland flight to London, then it was on to the jumbo for the long haul to Florida. The Masters is a great event, probably the ultimate theatre, but I was definitely *not* looking forward to coping with all the finicky rules and regulations. It's like nowhere else in the world in that respect.

The warm-up to our crack at the Masters began in similar fashion to that of 1989. First there was the Nestlé Invitation at the Bay Hill Club and Lodge in Orlando and then the Houston Open. I have never liked Orlando, a Mickey Mouse town, and we played golf to match.

At practice the mood and the form were definitely not good. Seve wasn't hitting the ball well and played terribly in the Pro Am. The brow darkened even more when we shot 77, five over, on the first day, including a nine on the eleventh: my fault – I gave him the wrong club.

The second day was almost as bad. An eight on the sixth with two balls in the water and a three over 75. We said goodbye to Orlando on 26 March with another nice early-morning start – a 6 am flight to Houston. I arrived at 9.30 and rang home to find Boro had lost 1–0. That finished the week off nicely. Missed the cut and Boro went down: I wasn't feeling happy.

Houston, however, has always been one of my favourite tournaments. Seve had some tickets to the NBA game featuring the Houston Rockets that night and we posed next to 7-foot-something Akeem the Dream, the Rockets' star centre. On occasions like this Seve can be the best of company. We would just talk about sport in general as two friends would, although I have to admit that if we went out for a meal it was always Seve who paid! It was a great night: the Rockets won and the relaxation seemed to do Seve the world of good, because he played really well in practice on the Tuesday. I had another good night out with Phil 'Wobbly' Morbey, Ian Woosnam's caddie, at The Park listening to a jazz pianist. Then some joker drew us for a 7.30 am start on the Thursday and I began to wonder where my next lie-in was coming from.

On the last day in Houston Seve got into contention and all of a sudden I was looking at my first win in America. Coming on to the seventeenth, we were facing a dogleg to the left followed by a second over water to the island green. He took a nine iron off the middle of the fairway for the second and just turned it over to the left. The ball finished up on top of the sleepers building up the left-hand side of the plateau. It was really a terrible shot and the hopes of a win died there and then, because he made a five to leave us one behind going up the last. A great putt on eighteen lipped the hole and that was it, we were tied third. He should have won but it wasn't a bad build-up to the Masters.

Augusta is one of those courses you can visit three or four times and still find it has surprises for you. You can make as many notes as you like, but there's still something you don't know. I haven't mastered it yet. Still, I tried to go through the routine, or as close to a routine as the organizers will allow. I had all the yardages from the previous years and nothing had changed, even the sprinklers were in the same place. We went up to register, played the course in practice, checked the greens and picked up my painter-and-decorator's outfit – my favourite gear! Perhaps I should audition for a part in *Space 2000* because that's what I feel like in that uniform.

Two over on the first day and it could have been a good round, but Seve putted awfully. With one four putt and several three putts, that was where the round was thrown away, because level par is not a bad score but he never got close with his putts. The greens were good as usual, fast, but he was holing absolutely nothing and it was the same old story on the Friday: plenty of chances and nothing going down in a 73. Saturday was better except for two bad drives on four and five, the second way into the trees, and on the last day he played well enough to finish tied seventh.

Now I look back on the National course and know

that because it is so demanding I should have worked hard and concentrated even harder because Seve was not. He wasn't there half the time. I should have been wary for both of us. I think if I could have done that he would have snapped out of it and we could have got going again. I've been to Augusta twice, which gives me twice as much experience as someone going there for the first time. I have the experience and know-how of two trips there but I know I'm still learning and perhaps always will be.

After buying some presents for the lads I went back out to the course for a leisurely walk round. It was a strange feeling being there almost alone and with everything so quiet and peaceful: like a battlefield after the last cannon had been fired. I met some of the guys from the BBC who were having their highly honoured media round and they kindly asked me to play sixteen and seventeen with them. I made two bogeys and now I know how Seve feels.

On the way home depression started to set in. I'd been away for three weeks and packed a lot of hard work into that time. I left Augusta at 8.30 am, Orlando at 3.15 pm. It took four flights to get home and I arrived at Heathrow at 7 in the morning. Which morning? I didn't really know. This was the glamorous life of a golf caddie – your player's down and so are you and the next tournament is only a week away.

At home there was just time to book for Madrid, phone Hugo Boss and ask for a new supply of shirts and have a round of golf down the road. Sixth place won me an Easter egg, so things couldn't be all that bad.

On 16 April it was back to the Seve homeland for the Cepsa Madrid Open at Puerta de Hierro. If the week before had been bad this was even worse – for both of us. I had had a bereavement at home, Uncle Fred on my mother's side, and I didn't get much sleep through thinking about it; that and the fact that my room-mate was snoring all night.

'Fed up' is too mild a term to describe our feelings and in the Pro Am it showed. We lost a ball completely on the third, then Seve played the wrong ball. I had decided not to tell him about the death at home. I didn't want to bother him but he had a black time anyway when the tournament got going. A 76 and a 72 and a missed cut is a disaster anywhere; in Spain, however, it's worse than murder for a national hero.

One week later we were at Club de Campo Madrid for the Peugeot Spanish Open and the weather decided to get in tune with our mood and Seve's form. We practised in the freezing cold and it actually started to snow. Snow in Spain in April: what next? I was standing there like a snowman with my feet and fingers going solid and wondering, 'What exactly am I doing here?'

But, as if on cue, Seve picked us both up with a win in the Pro Am. Talk about swings and roundabouts! The fifteenth was an incredible hole for him. He hit a drive into the trees and was laid right up by a tree trunk. He played out 120 metres left-handed and then chipped in from 20 metres for a remarkable birdie. Again I had to ask, 'Who else could have played that?' Unfortunately, the tournament itself was more downhill than up: plus two on the first day and a 70 on the second to make the cut on even par but eight under was leading. We had 68 and a 69 to finish and tied on sixth after the four days.

It made a pleasant change to get back to Britain and the Benson and Hedges International at St Mellion, Cornwall, the course that Jack (Nicklaus) built. Lesley met me at Gatwick when I flew in from Madrid and we stayed at East Looe, a lovely place that reminds me a little of Whitby. I measured the course on Tuesday and, after meeting the famous Bond Brothers who own it, Seve had a good practice on the Wednesday. He thought his game was getting better and told me so, but in the Pro Am it didn't look that way. Eddie Large was our playing partner and cheered us up a bit; he even managed two nett eagles. We've been out with Eddie a few times and he's a bundle of laughs. He can't help it if he's a Manchester City fan – we all have our problems.

Tee-off time for the tournament was 8.10 am and I was up at 6.15. The course was dry and firm and the ball was bouncing everywhere. Seve wasn't happy, wasn't enjoying it and not into playing golf at all. Occasionally he took it out on me, but it was nothing to start crying about. On Saturday he played really badly, a 77, and only two birdies in the last three holes saved a genuine disaster. He was twice in the water on Sunday and Monday was another bad day. He tied fortieth after some pretty dismal golf. I didn't know what was wrong with him and the only hope was to keep plugging away and hope that he'd come out of it. Still, we hadn't had the 'major disaster' that Seve said would spell the beginning of the end. But I knew it wasn't far away.

The Lancia Martini Italian Open, held in Milan, is one of the few tournaments Seve has never won. Mike Tadd, the European representative for Titleist, was there at the hotel and put his briefcase down for a second by the side of the reception desk. Someone walked off with it and all the company facts and figures. I'm not that keen on Italy either.

Meanwhile, back on the roller coaster: we had a bad

practice day, but then we won the Pro Am with a five under 68. It was another false dawn, because Seve scored a first-day 75 and there was real trouble on the Friday when we were plus four after the eleventh and I was contemplating another early flight home. Then he finished the last seven like this: birdie twelve, par thirteen, eagle fourteen, par fifteen, birdie sixteen, birdie seventeen and par eighteen. What could I say! One minute we were in a right hole and then he just produces an incredible burst like that. For the umpteenth time that season I said to myself, 'This time he *has* turned the corner.'

On the Saturday it poured down but a 66 lifted the clouds a bit, and on Sunday he managed a 69 without putting well. Tied fifth wasn't bad in the end, particularly when I look back and think that after twenty-nine holes he was four over. To finish off the week I experienced another exciting chapter in the life of a caddie. I decided to change my flight from London to Manchester so that Lesley could pick me up at Ringway, but then I discovered that flight was delayed and I didn't touch down until 9.15 that night. Definitely not too keen on Italy.

Officially I was due a week off but, as so often happens, found that there weren't enough days in the week. After trying to book for Nice and Paris later in the year I had only Friday in which to try to lay a concrete foundation for a garden shed at home and pack for the States at the same time. On Sunday I was off to Washington for the Kemper Open but overslept, got the departure time wrong and finished up with five minutes to get out and to the airport.

Kemper was another mini-disaster: plus two and Seve didn't play well at all. We made another bad start and went on from there, and by this time I'd forgotten what it was like to have a good start to a tournament. He missed the cut by one shot and suddenly I found I was in hot water. He blamed me for not telling him the cut was plus two.

'If you had told me that I would have made the cut,' he said. Then, amazingly, he added, 'I'm not really telling you this to make you feel bad.'

Perhaps he expected me to be happy after hearing that. Needless to say, I wasn't. By now I had done some sums and had worked out that I was actually paying for the privilege of caddying for Seve. After three weeks in America we were on a terrible streak with just one tournament, the Butler National Open at Oakbrook, Illinois, in which to try to find some form before the US Open. But accommodation, food and travel in the US is definitely not cheap and I had to find it all. Who would have thought that carrying a bag for Seve Ballesteros would actually cost me money?

Practice on the Monday was good and then on Tuesday I saw yet another side to Seve. He caddied for Carmen, who is quite a tidy little player, in the wives' tournament and really got into it. Carmen played really well and they finished second or third to win a team prize. How much was down to Seve and his club selection and his yardages, I don't know. All I do know is that I didn't see her muttering at him when she played up short!

After a no return in the Pro Am, we were back in the basement on the first day of the tournament. He shot a 77, five over, and the despair was etched all over his face. At the time I felt he had no confidence on the golf course and there was little I could do to help except try to encourage him from time to time. I was feeling the strain for him and it was sad, terribly sad, to see him struggling like that. He seemed to be playing well in practice, but then seemed to leave it all there.

It looked like another missed cut, but I was wrong again. He shot three birdies in the last eight holes, including a birdie on eighteen, to make the last two days and I again hoped that this was the thing that would spark him off. But it wasn't. He was four over on the Saturday and on Sunday we finished down the field among the also-rans. I didn't feel confident about the US Open.

The Open that year was at Medinah, Chicago, a wooded course with plenty of water, plenty of traps for the unwary, which naturally, on our then form, included us. As we were already in Chicago all I had to do on 11 June was change hotels to move a bit closer to Medinah, and when I arrived Seve was already at practice. We went out with Olazabal and Sandy on the Monday and on the Tuesday there was a pretty heavy foursome of Seve, Curtis Strange, Greg Norman and Peter Jacobsen.

It was while we were out on the course that Seve told me he was going to pull out of the French Open at Chantilly: a good decision, because at the time he was as down as anyone could be and I felt the break would do him good since he wasn't enjoying his golf. His mood of resignation to fate was confirmed on the Wednesday when, after practice in the morning, he told me to take the afternoon off – unheard of! I just wasn't used to this but managed to get my lucky streak going again – temporarily – by driving down to Arlington Racecourse and winning $100. I'd seen Arlington on TV but in the flesh it was something else, all done out in marble, and it was a fine experience to see one of the great racecourses of the world. The afternoon off seemed to relax me a little. Could I carry the luck into the tournament? No chance!

Following an early walk around to check all the pins, Seve started off poorly with a 73, one over. The putts still wouldn't go in and, even though his 69 on the second day looked promising, there was still no confidence there. At three under we were technically there or thereabouts, but a good start was vital on the third day.

After twelve months of waiting here it was – the major disaster! After getting a good par on the first we came to the second and the hole I will remember for the rest of my life. It's a shortish par three over water. Seve was in a terrible, testy mood.

'What club is it?' he asked.

I looked at the yardage and I could see there was a strong wind blowing from right to left and I also considered what clubs other players had taken all week. 'Six iron, I decided.'

But he hit a terrible shot with it, the ball took a low, flat hook and never looked like carrying the water. Splash!

Seve blew his top completely – it was all my fault, naturally. I gave him another ball and he knocked it on the green – with the same club – and as we were walking away he said, 'Well, that certainly won't happen again.'

I knew there and then that our relationship was about to end. I sensed that the sack was just round the corner and, daft as it seems, all I could feel was relief. I really started to relax after that. I tried to encourage him, to get him back into the tournament, but it had gone.

With the way things had worked out that season, I knew I was going to get the blame eventually and this was it. The excuse was the club choice, but then again Seve didn't give me any help on the selection and really played an awful shot. Other players with less power had reached the green with a six even with a strong wind. With a five he would have made the green all right, but on the second at Medinah the last place you want to be is behind the flag because it's a big sloping green. Even now I don't know if it was the wrong club or the right club because he just never hit the ball. I was wrong at the Masters but I don't think I was wrong at Medinah.

Life became pretty intolerable during the remainder of the round. After giving me some stick Seve more or less stopped talking to me; or at least, when he did talk, it was just to have another go as he marched along. Of course we missed the cut, and the moment I had been waiting for arrived when we got back to the clubhouse and start to stow the gear away.

'Well, I think that's it, Ian.'

I said, 'Fine. Thanks very much for everything you've done for me.'

I packed the bag, took it to his car and he drove off into the sunset with Carmen.

In a situation like this there was only one thing to do and I took the time-honoured remedy of a few beers. When I was lying in bed the next morning, trying to come round, the hotel room phone rang. It was Seve. For the first time in two years he had rung *me*. Now he showed what a big man he is.

'Ian, I want you to carry on from Monte Carlo. I know my form is bad but I shouldn't blame you for it.'

It showed me there is a big heart inside there as well, that he has feelings. Maybe he was right and maybe he was wrong. I knew things had not gone well and I had been expecting the sack or a mutual parting. I also knew that our decision to get back together was only temporary, but I agreed to carry on until he could get fixed up with another caddie.

The details didn't take long to finalize. When I got home I talked to Joe Collet and he asked me to ring Seve that Thursday to discuss the rest of the year. Seve came up with this game plan: I would caddie for him for the rest of the year – OK by me; I wouldn't be going to America with him – even better by me; I wouldn't have the bag at the British Open at St Andrews – I wasn't over the moon about that, but he explained he wanted to try again with big brother Vicente, so fair enough. I relaxed with a couple of weeks off.

When I arrived in Monte Carlo on 2 July it was business as usual. Seve was right as rain with me and there were no hangovers from Medinah. In many ways the talk had done us both a world of good. If nothing else it had cleared the air, and all I thought of was doing my best for my boss for the rest of the year. I tried to put everything else out of my mind.

Monte Carlo, as it happened, did turn into something special. I actually saw Seve smile again. On the first day we shot a three under 66, but on the second he managed his first hole in one in tournament golf. After fifteen seasons Seve had an ace! It's a plateau green with the hole out of sight and he took an eight iron. We didn't even see the ball go into the hole and there wasn't exactly a roar of delight from the gallery because there were only about seven spectators there and three of them were marshals. It was probably the poorest crowd of the year for Seve's big first. His reaction, too, was quite subdued: there was no jig of joy or anything, just a little smile and then on with the job. Perhaps the hole in one did give him a bit of a lift, because he shot a 63 on the Friday and played the best golf I'd seen from him for a long time. A top-ten finish was a definite improvement.

While I was out in America for the US Open I had met up with Jerry Pate again and arranged to work for him at the Bells Scottish Open at Gleneagles, Seve being at home. Staying with Lesley at Mrs Toms' up at Auchterarder would be a nice break for me, and Jerry, who was making a comeback after a serious shoulder injury and the surgery to try to cure it, is always good company.

A past US Open and US PGA winner, Jerry Pate has been around for a long time and I've seen a lot of him over the years during his stints as a commentator for ABC. He's a happy-go-lucky sort of bloke from Macon, Georgia, and well known for eccentricities. After a win in one tournament back in the States he took a run and a dive into the lake bordering the eighteenth green. As long as he didn't expect me to follow suit if he won at Gleneagles !

Jerry played quite well in the Pro Am, shooting a 77 in a strong wind, but his touch wasn't there on the greens. He was playing with Ian Baker-Finch, who demonstrated in a very amusing fashion just what life for a top player would be like without a caddie. Peering down the thirteenth fairway towards the hole, he said, 'I think I'll just lay up short of that bunker.' I was standing there watching and saying nothing, and sure enough he played up short with a three wood.

I couldn't resist it then. 'I don't think you would have reached that bunker, Ian,' I said. 'It's all of 420 yards away.'

Ian just burst out laughing. One up for the caddies!

Although Jerry couldn't get going at Gleneagles he decided he had a chance of getting into the Open at St Andrews and we set off for Lundin links and the pre-qualifying tournament. With five holes to play in the first round, Jerry was going along nicely and I was beginning to think I would have a bag in the Open after all, but then he had a horrendous triple bogey on seventeen and we finished one over. It spoiled what had been a good day because he is a great guy to get on with and I was really starting to enjoy golf again. On the Monday he started birdie, birdie, but then four-putted the third. We had plenty of chances yet didn't hole anything until the twelfth and he struggled home to finish 142 and three shots off an Open spot. It now looked definite that I would be without a bag at St Andrews. But Jerry had been a treat to work with and he really looked after me well.

The satellite TV channel BSB (as it was then known, before its amalgamation with Sky Channel) had asked me a couple of weeks before to get in touch if I wasn't going to caddie in the Open, and when the first round began at St Andrews I found myself in their commentary box. It was a weird feeling to be on the outside looking in. I was doing little pieces on the play and giving a sort of caddie's eye view of what went on. I also got invited to the sportswriters' dinner for the northern section of the *Mail on Sunday*, courtesy of writers Peter Higgs and Bob Cass – a fine pair of reprobates, but then I get on well with all the golfing Press.

Guys like Frank Clough of the *Sun* have been good to me, and Martin Hardy of the *Daily Express* has been up to Redcar for a round of golf with me. I've always tried to help the Press where Seve was concerned but they have never tried to overstep the mark – they have always appreciated that there are confidentialities. There have been no attempts to dig the dirt on Seve, and not just because there is no dirt to dig. The golfing Press know the rules of the game and the only minor bit of friction occurred when I was away at players' school and a newspaper rang Damon at home trying to quiz him about the date of Seve's wedding. Damon just told them basically to take a long walk off a short pier and that was the end of that.

At St Andrews I went up to the house where Seve was staying to wish him luck and Carmen, too, because she was heavily pregnant and about to give birth at any time. Everywhere I went at St Andrews the crowds were very kind to me, coming up and asking, 'Why aren't you with *him*?' I even had to sign a few autographs. I enjoyed a good night out at the *Golf World* barbecue and for the first time in a long while I was having a really relaxing time at a Major, although I still couldn't get away from Seve and his nightmare. Whatever was wrong, brother Vicente had no cure for it either and he went out at half-way. Really it was just a continuation of the way things had gone for Seve all year, with or without me.

While I was up in Scotland I had a word with Gordon J. Brand about working for him at the KLM Dutch Open at Zandvoort, another tournament Seve had crossed off his list for that year. Roy Holland was off to caddie for Brian Waites in the Volvo British Seniors at Turnberry and Gordon was without a caddie for that week. Even though I knew I would have to put up with the awful Brand jokes, I was looking forward to trying to give him a bit of a boost because he had not had a good year.

First round, and he started bogey, bogey. 'Where have I seen this before?' I thought. He seemed to lack confidence with his putter but he birdied sixteen, one of the hardest holes on the course, and finished with two more. The next day was what you might call a bogey-birdie day for a 70 and plus four, but the day after it started to come together for him and his 67 tied us for eighth. One more good round would have given Gordon the finish he badly needed, but he shot 73. Tied fifteenth wasn't total disaster and Gordon paid me a nice compliment at the end in saying what a good job I'd done for him and hopefully I'd work for him again some day. It cheered me up no end, because preying on my mind all the time was the thought of going back to good old America the week after with Seve.

When I had seen Seve at the British Open he had had a change of heart about my work schedule and decided that I would go to America with him for a crack at the US PGA. Frankly it was the last place I wanted to go and I had told him so at St Andrews. I said I couldn't justify going there if I had to find my own air fares because there was a good chance of my losing more money. It did not seem like a good idea. But he agreed to pay my flight out and there was a nice bonus in the form of a ride back on Concorde: Seve had two tickets and offered me one.

Even this couldn't banish the feeling of dread in my mind, however. There was the Federal Express and St Jude Classic to start with in Memphis, and then the PGA itself at Birmingham, Alabama. I knew it was going to be very hot and humid and there was still no sign of Seve coming out of his slump. What's more, I knew the PGA was going to be tough at Shoal Creek because, as for every PGA was going to e tough at Shoal Creek because, as for every PGA course, the rough is set up thick. It's the same every time. I could sniff disaster in the air.

I got upgraded from tourist to club class on the flight out to Memphis on 31 July, a good start, but then we were back in the doldrums. Knocked out at the third hole in the pre-tournament shoot-out, Seve then had a no return in the pro Am. The confidence was still missing and in the tournament it was the same old story. A 74 on the first day, three over, was poor by Seve's standards, and on the Friday there was still no heart, no spark. It was as if he were playing by memory and missing the cut was almost a relief.

Flying down to Birmingham, I began to feel a bit desperate, totally lost. I felt there was nothing else I could do to help him. You tried your best and kept trying, but nothing changed: certainly not his mood. On the thirteenth hole at Shoal Creek he was putting off the fringe and I was holding the flag ready to put it back in the hole. He charged the putt past the hole and then turned on me. This time it was my fault for not putting the flag back in the hole fast enough. After that he was really bad-tempered, muttering and moaning all the way round to seventeen where, with a shot over the water, almost inevitably he dunked it in. He should have carried it easily – there was no trouble as far as I was concerned – but it was down to me again and there was another major blow-up.

By this time I was sick to my back teeth and came off the course muttering and cursing. I decided enough was enough, put the yardage book in the top pocket of his bag so that he would find it easily, put the clubs away and went back round the front for a couple of beers.

When Seve appeared he asked, 'Do you want a lift back to the hotel?'

'Yes, because I want a talk with you in the car.'

On the drive back he chatted about this and that, but all the time he knew there was something wrong with me.

Eventually I came out with it: 'I don't want to caddie for you tomorrow.'

That really shocked him. 'You can't do that! It's just pure frustration at the moment, Ian. Sleep on it, think it over.'

It's a sad thing to say now, but I really didn't want to caddie for him the next day. If he had lost heart, then so had I. Everything over the last twelve months had caught up with me and this was the breaking point. I'd given it my best shot and it obviously wasn't good enough. But I couldn't do this to him and in the end I said, 'OK, I'll be there tomorrow.'

And so we went out again on the Friday, ready for more punishment, but on the way to the tee, to his credit, he said, 'Come on, let's have a go and see if we can get back into this tournament.'

It was wishful thinking. For the first five we battled away and just missed a birdie chance, but after that nothing went right – the ball was going all over the place. Another two-day tournament.

At the end we trooped off together and as far as I was concerned it was the end. It was the NM English Open at The Belfry the week after, but I didn't really have the urge to caddie there. At the travel agency on the course I managed to change the now unnecessary Concorde tickets to two first-class and off we went.

Now despite what happens in a tournament we have always remained friends off the course and one way this relationship was never going to end was with spilled blood and hasty words. The decision was made mutually: The Belfry would be our last round together. we decided to tell no one but agreed that the ideal way to go out would be with a win.

'It's probably for the best,' said Seve, 'and this way we can stay friends without anyone losing out.'

And this was what I wanted, an amicable rather than acrimonious parting. I rationalized that there comes a time when every relationship has to end and this was the best time for ours. Now I could relax and enjoy the flight and the creature comforts of first-class air travel. There was nothing really to celebrate but the champagne still tasted good.

As I still had all the yardages from the Ryder Cup, I could approach The Belfry and the NM English Open in a more laid-back fashion than usual, and Seve was in a similar mood when I met him on the Sunday. We dined together as friends and then went off to the pictures – Arnold Schwarzenegger in *Total Recall*: very violent.

In Seve I saw signs of the old sparkle and, sure enough, on the Tuesday he won the shoot-out and then posted a steady 70 in the Pro Am. Even par on the first day left us tied third and he played steady on Friday to stay in the same position. Then, on the Sunday, he went berserk with six birdies in the last six holes and at third on our own we were in with a good chance. It would be nice to go out with a victory!

By the fourteenth on the final round we were up with the leaders and an 18-inch putt would tie us for the lead. He missed it and from then on in we were struggling. On seventeen he hit a drive over the corner and it caught a tree. A good shot out saw us just short of the green, but then a poor chip landed us with a six and that was it. After that we just went through the motions.

So we arrived at eighteen, our last hole together, and all sort of things were going through my mind. The greatest feeling, I have to admit, was one of relief, relief that all the pressure was about to be lifted. A great drive, a super second to 8 feet, but a missed putt for birdie just about summed up the last twelve months: golf played the way only Seve can play it some of the time and missed opportunities and frustration the rest of the time. It was a pity, really, not to leave with a win, which is what we had both wanted, but fourth place wasn't too bad a way to bow out.

I went slowly through the ritual for the last time, packing everything up, taking the clubs round to the car, handing them over. As always, Seve was dashing off to another airport. I said, 'Thanks for everything' once again and 'I hope everything goes well with the baby.' Seve didn't say much. He was in a rush and there were a lot of people around, so there was a quick handshake and that was it.

We did, however, get one win that week – or rather, Andy Prodger and I did. It was the Caddies' Championship at The Belfry, and although I had no clubs I decided to enter in the section for non-Association members and Andy agreed to carry my bag. No expense was spared, with £5 plus a percentage if I won the £30 first prize. I had one of Seve's old putters and Wilson the golf club manufacturers loaned me some clubs, including a Firestick driver with a whale head, and off we went. It was a windy day but I managed to keep my shots under the breeze and Andy was helping, encouraging me as he once did Nick Faldo, although of course he probably never called Nick some of the names he called me on the way round.

We heard that 77 was the best score in, and although I was going nicely along at four over, I made a real mess of the fifteenth with a double bogey six. On the sixteenth, which is a downhill dogleg, I said to Andy, 'I must do something here.' I launched into the ball with this whale-head driver, almost drove the green and then chipped in from the fringe for an eagle! Andy and I were doing a lap of honour round the sixteenth green, and at four over all I had to do was par in. A three on seventeen and a par on the last left me with a 76 and a win by one shot. At 18½ per cent of the £30 prize money, Andy got the biggest percentage of his life!

After our last round together I had to come to terms with life without Seve and it was difficult. It was going to take time to get over and Andy said he had the same problems when Faldo sacked him. I had to try to get my life back to something like normal, but it was hard, after spending so long in a pressure cooker, to come out and relax. Still, I had to carry on earning a living.

Steen Tinning had asked me to work for him at the Swiss Open at Crans and I was delighted to help. Steen is potentially a great player, but at the time was making a comeback after being badly hurt in a car smash. He broke his arm and had been out for five months. I had originally helped him get his card at Walton Heath and now it was a case of just trying to help him get his game back together.

At Crans I spoke to Seve and congratulated him on the birth of his son, Baldomero, but I still felt a bit lost. There was no Pro Am, of course, and Steen missed the cut in the Swiss. He started with an eagle on the par five first, but after that it was all downhill and he decided to pull out of the European Open at Sunningdale the following week. Seve didn't have a good tournament either and was rebuked for alleged slow play. He blamed this on the lack of stewards.

At Sunningdale the Press had found out about the big split and asked the obvious question: 'Was it amicable?' I told them it was. I got a job carrying John Morgan's bag and *he* missed the cut, so I was finding myself with a lot of time on my hands.

The year was slowly winding down. On 10 September I flew out to Copenhagen to carry for Steen and stayed in his apartment. He had another mediocre tournament, but I broke new ground again on the last day when Budget Cars, in return for a few photographs for publicity purposes, loaned me a Ferrari to go to the airport. Pete Coleman can keep his Porsche!

I wanted to spend the rest of the year coming down from all the adrenalin spent with Seve, yet found I was kept busy with more commentary jobs. I covered the Suntory Matchplay at Wentworth and the Dunhill Cup at St Andrews, and perhaps this is the direction my career will take in the future when the old legs start to go. Commentary I found was a different way of relaxing and everyone I came across gave me bags of encouragement – Clive Clark, whom I would bump into on the fairways, Renton Laidlaw, all of them.

At the Suntory I was actually doing the driving for the Press, but Radio 5 asked me in to commentate on the final day. I went out with Tony Adamson and thoroughly enjoyed myself and found myself at the Dunhill Cup for the conclusion there. I discovered I had to learn some new skills: on radio golf commentary you have to walk and talk at the same time and there were three of us – Tony, the man with the sound pack and myself – glued together and guiding each other along as we came to the bridge at the Swilkin Burn at St Andrews. Now you try walking across there holding hands three abreast ... our laughter came loud and clear over the airwaves!

Looking back to the day I first took up a player's bag, who would ever have thought I would finish up working for the greatest golfer in the world and enjoying the success I did with him – one Major and eight other wins? The memories will always be there, and they came alive again when a letter landed on the carpet from Seve with a note from Carmen thanking me for all my efforts. My heart warmed to both of them.

It's not good to see a great player being so down. Greg Norman was in the same state at the Dunhill Cup and Sandy Lyle has been through it too. It was awful to watch Seve struggling that last summer and hard to put my finger on the reasons. It was just something indefinable that everyone goes through. I want to see him back and firing on all cylinders and I'm sure it will happen. The game of golf needs a successful Seve Ballesteros – almost as much as he needs golf.